City on Seven Hills

Gareth Hiebert, early in his St. Paul newspaper career, *circa* 1940.

City
on
Seven
Hills

Columns of
Oliver Towne

▲ ▲ ▲ ▲ ▲ ▲ ▲

by Gareth Hiebert

POGO PRESS

ISBN 1-880654-17-2

Library of Congress Catalogue Card No. 99-62981

Permission from Walker Lundy, Editor, to reprint articles
contained in the
St. Paul Dispatch and Pioneer Press
is gratefully acknowledged.

Ink drawings by Julie A. Hiebert
appear on pages 12, 45, and 98.

Permission from Bill Boudewyns, Editor, to reprint an
article contained in Skyway News is gratefully acknowledged.

Pre-press by North Star Press of St. Cloud, Inc.

Printing by Versa Press, Inc.

Published by
Pogo Press, Incorporated
Four Cardinal Lane
St. Paul, Minnesota 55127

A WORD FROM THE PUBLISHER

Geographers map St. Paul's boundaries and streets, and they will verify that it was built upon seven hills with the names Baptist, Capitol, Cathedral, Ramsey, Dayton's Bluff, West Side, and St. Clair. Historians write about St. Paul's notable events and famous people. Artists capture St. Paul's picturesque vistas and views. But to know the neighborhoods of St. Paul you need to read the newspapers and discover, as Gareth Hiebert did, those hills and amidst them, the city's ups and downs.

Newspaper columnists have captured the soul of the saintly city for decades. They've recorded the changes, the sounds and even the smells of Minnesota's capital. They have served as witnesses to change, to small-scale triumphs, and even to occasional tragedies that have marked the city's first 150 years.

As readers of the St. Paul *Pioneer Press*, or the *Dispatch* or the *Daily News* we may not always have realized that the "Paul Light" column was really written first by Howard Kahn and later by Roy Dunlap, Jr., or that "Hawf & Hawf" was P. J. Hoffstrom, but we knew their columns would tell us something we didn't know about the town that was their beat and our home.

Even after newspaper columnists stop writing their columns, their words remain as records of a past time and place that prove useful to future historians. Want to know about the West Side in the 1920s? Read Bill Hoffman. Curious about Grand Avenue? Find James Taylor Dunn's stories.

In a recent New Yorker magazine article about the late Chicago newspaperman Mike Royko, author Hendrik Hertzberg described Royko as a "soul-of-the-city" columnist. S.O.C.'s, Hertzberg wrote, were a special breed on city papers, establishing a national tradition that stretched from H. L. Mencken in Baltimore to Mike Royko of Chicago, Herb Caen of San Francisco, and Jimmy Breslin in New York City.

But for a look at St. Paul in general, or for a warm-hearted, closeup view, there is no better S.O.C. than the man who later became both a tour guide and a teacher of St. Paul history and who was for more than thirty years, as his pen name aptly puts it, Oliver Towne.

PREFACE

Readers of the St. Paul *Dispatch* on November 1, 1954 found a new column on the back page, called Oliver Towne, which some translated as All Over Town, and many thought it was a new staff member. Hundreds never did make the connection. So that for 34 years when I wrote this column, I was known as Oliver Towne and even cashed checks with that name.

Even now I meet people who call me Oliver.

Columnists and columns come in all shapes and sizes and subject matter. Some are political, others opinionated, and there are gossip columns, entertainment, business and humor columns.

Mine was human interest. I wrote about the drama of the city, its charm, the big and little people, the places and things. I tried to capture the color, the life of the city. And in 34 years I never wavered from that theme. My friends were mayors, bankers, street people. They belonged to the generation of the 1950s, '60s, and '70s.

Writing a column is stressful and demanding. You use notes from people, phone calls from people, and letters. In my role, I often went out on the site to interview, to describe a scene, to listen to the sounds of the city and use them.

When I started, I had 10 columns in the drawer and on the day I retired in 1986 I had 10 columns in the drawer. The earlier columns were in the *Dispatch*, the later ones were in the *Pioneer Press*.

Like the famed foreign correspondent of the 1920s Walter Duranty, who "Wrote as I Pleased," I had pretty much carte blanche. But I always was required to submit every column to the managing editor, who seldom changed a word.

I came to the *Pioneer Press* and *Dispatch* in 1939 at the age of 18. My home town was New Ulm, Minnesota, where I wrote for the New Ulm *Daily Journal* during my last year in High School and for one year after that. I then came to St. Paul for a job on the *Pioneer Press*, covering the University of Minnesota while I was going to journalism school. I worked nights and went to class days and was graduated in the spring of 1943, just in time to be called to duty in the Army.

I survived the Battle of the Bulge and the battle of Germany as an infantry man and later served as public relations chief of the 84th Infantry Division. I retired after 34 years in the army reserves as a Lieutenant Colonel.

From 1946 until I became Oliver Towne, I was a feature writer and assistant city editor of the *Pioneer Press*.

There will never be another Oliver Towne column in the St. Paul papers, but I have been succeeded by some worthy writers who have great affection for the city. Among them is Don Boxmeyer, whose columns capture the feel of the city and its interesting people.

I was married for 51 years to my college sweetheart—Janet— who died of cancer in 1997. We raised four children, two girls and two boys, one of whom is a United Airlines captain and the other a financial planner with American Express. My daughters are— one a school teacher and mother of two—and the second a computer whiz. Janet lived to see the last of four grandchildren.

A number of years ago some of my earlier columns were published in two books by The North Central Publishing Company. They are now long out of print. This new book republishes a number of those columns, and adds some others.

Often late at night I reread these stories of the city which has been my home of 59 years and whose story I have chronicled with love.

Gareth Hiebert
St. Paul, Minnesota
April 8, 1999

DEDICATION

This book is dedicated to Janet, my wife of 51 years, who was my
cheerleader and shared the wonderful adventures of life and
column writing that were ours.

OTHER BOOKS BY GARETH HIEBERT

The Man on the Street Visits a St. Paul Public School. St. Paul: *St. Paul Dispatch* and *Pioneer Press.* 1958.

Saint Paul is my beat. St. Paul, Minnesota: The North Central Publishing Company. 1958.

Once Upon a Towne. St. Paul, Minnesota: The North Central Publishing Company. 1959.

Oliver's Travels. St. Paul, Minnesota: The North Central Publishing Company. 1973.

A Dream Comes True. Memories of Mantorville. Mantorville, Minnesota: I. Pappas. 1978.

My Years at St. Olaf. From Melby to Mel. Northfield, Minnesota: St. Olaf College. 1988.

Little Canada, A Voyageur's Vision: History of Little Canada. Stillwater, Minnesota: Croixside Press. 1989.

The Dahcotah History Hotel. 1859 to 1972. Lake Mills, Iowa: Stoyles Graphic Services. 1989.

Fragments. The Art of Lloyd Herfindahl. Aurora, Illinois: Aurora University. 1994.

CONTENTS

St. Paul People

Artist Opts for Quiet Life

In nice weather, people come to Rice Park by the dozens to sit with their bag lunches on the oval concrete steps around the huge fountain sculpture called "The Source." They admire it and watch children on hot summer days daringly jump into the pool and splash near the figure of the woman, whom the sculptor called "the source of all life."

In the evening, with the lights playing across the park from the Ordway and Landmark, the splashing fountain takes on the luster of a park in Paris or a plaza in Rome. The people read carefully the inscription on the plaque opposite fastened to the water fountain, the one that tells how the Women's Institute gave this fountain sculpture to the city. But nowhere do they learn the name of the man who created perhaps the city's most-viewed outdoor sculpture.

The name Alonzo "Lonnie" Hauser is not visible. He never signed his most famous piece of work when he finished it in the early 1960s.

This blithe spirit founded the Macalester art department and once was barker for Gypsy Rose Lee's side show; had a magnetism that attracted "women in every town," as he used to say; created nude sculptures that earned him the sobriquet of St. Paul's

1

"Canova," and is the father of flamenco guitar players Tony and Mike Hauser and the one-time husband of ballet and dance impresario Nancy Hauser.

Lonnie is living these days in a room of St. Olaf Lutheran residence in Minneapolis "among a lot of old women" who are a far cry from the voluptuous beauties with whom he admittedly consorted all his life and used as models for his sculpture and paintings.

That's where I found him the other day, at the age of 76. The recipe for carrying youth into old age that he once expressed to me—roaming the country like a lone eagle, painting cities and towns, a land sailor with a romantic liaison in every port—had proved fickle.

His son, Tony, was there, as was a longtime friend, St. Paul artist Paul Kramer.

I told Lonnie that his "Source" was the most popular sculpture in town because so many people come and sit around it and read or eat their lunches and chat.

That made him happy but, he says, he still thought his two favorite public works were the 16-foot stone figure of Christ on the outside façade of St. Paul's United Church of Christ, at Summit and Milton, and the little mermaid sitting in the lily pad of the pool outside the Veterans Service building.

There was large controversy about her nudity when he unveiled it back in the 1950s. For a long time, the mechanism opening and closing the lily leaf remained shut.

"Then, people began to discover Rodin and Canova's 'Cupid and Psyche' in the Louvre and David's 'Bather' on canvas, and *Playboy* magazine," he says. "I hope people can see my little nymph. A girl at Macalester was the model. I wonder what ever happened to her?"

"Hey," he said, "remember the day you and I took a sauna in my sauna on the farm alongside Highway 49 in Dakota County?"

I remembered. The invitation followed a column I'd written about his work.

Not long afterward, the Dayton company bought the land for a good sum, and Lonnie used some of it to buy the three-story Masonic building in Prescott, Wisconsin.

The next time I saw him, he had opened his studio there and met Cotton Mather, University of Minnesota geographer and humorist who had a Western art shop down the street. Lonnie had just finished sculpting a tombstone with a phony inscription, which Mather passed off as the grave of an Indian chief right in his back yard. It was a tourist attraction for the gullible.

Lonnie studied art and sculpture in Paris and New York City with the luminaries of the day, taught at Carleton College and then came to Macalester. But the professorial air was not his bag.

He carved a portrait of Gypsy Rose Lee, then met her when she brought her revue to the Minnesota State Fair in 1949. Her husband, Julio de Diego, also an artist and barker for the show, wanted to go back to New York City. So Lonnie filled in at Topeka, Kansas.

"Working with Gypsy and all those beautiful gals was really a good antidote for the ivy-twined college life," he told me back in 1978 when he came to town for a big show of his paintings at the old Osborne Gallery on Grand Avenue.

If he had to do it all over again, Lonnie says he'd still opt for sculpting pretty girls, especially nudes, "which I sold by the gross."

"After all these centuries, the girls are still a subject of interest," he says, in a masterful understatement.

"And I knew a lot of them."

"Honey Boy" Helping Santa Round Up Toys

Hayward Toussaint, also the light-middleweight boxing legend known as "Honey Boy" Conroy, stands in ramrod splendor just inside the front door of the St. Vincent de Paul "used goods general store" at 461 Fort Road. He is wearing his blue uniform with the visored cap and the shield that marks him as a security guard, concierge, greeter and patter of little heads.

It is Saturday morning in the hectic days before Christmas. This is the only day of the week that Honey Boy adds his lofty size, polish and prestige to the St. Vincent de Paul store. And when he does, he gives it the same class enjoyed by shoppers at Bloomingdale's, Tiffany's and Cartier's in New York City.

Honey Boy has the aplomb of the doorman at The St. Paul Hotel and the regal bearing of royalty, which he is.

"And his being here—even one day a week—adds style, even at the 25-cent counter and at the 50-cent and $2 clothing racks," says the store's Mike Ettel.

"I'd make it every day," says Honey Boy, who donates his presence and appearance.

"But Saturday is the big day when they need a little traffic direction and questions answered."

Shoplifting is not a problem because everything is almost free anyway.

Honey Boy wears the same uniform he does two nights a week when he patrols the Metro Square building for Gary and Alex Tankenoff.

It is almost as formal as the official uniform with brass buttons which Honey Boy wore for 26 years as the greeter, concierge and big smiler at the elevator banks at City Hall.

But it is a great deal more ostentatious than the pair of boxing trunks and gloves he wore in the 1920s when he was setting records—a world record of 15 fights in three months. He boxed in

213 fights, 80 of them amateur and the rest professional until he hung up his gloves in 1938 as the uncrowned light-heavyweight champion.

The paychecks were as low as $50 a fight and as high as $1,100.

"Every day, you'd find us working out in the old Rosewood Gym in the Hamm Building basement—me and fighters like Jim Beatty, Mike Collins, Johnny Salvador and Jack Dorn. And I can't remember them all," he said.

Honey Boy had the added luster of his name and heritage.

"Now, that name Honey Boy was hung on me by some gal who told me Toussaint wasn't no fit name for a boxer. There was a big hockey player then named Tony Conroy and this gal said, 'You ought to be known as Honey Boy Conroy. If that's a good name for a hockey player, it's good enough for a boxer.' That's how I got the name and it stuck all my life."

Honey Boy's other name echoes some historic intrigue and prestige that perhaps not even the striped trousered doormen at Fortnum & Mason in London can match.

He stems from that branch of the Toussaints, who produced the "Hero of Haiti," Toussaint L'Ouverture, who freed the slaves and brought freedom to that French colony.

His unofficial rule lasted only from 1795 to 1802, when Napoleon, frightened by reports of the island's strike for independence, sent ships and troops to put down the unrest. L'Ouverture was captured and, later, killed.

"My great-great-grandfather was his brother," says Honey Boy. "L'Ouverture meant 'ruler' to him. I have traced his past and mine. He had come to Haiti from North Africa as a slave. He had four sons, and one of them was my great-great-grandfather—I can't find out which—who managed to escape to New Orleans when Napoleon annihilated Toussaint.

"I never rightly knew all the facts because I was a runaway; came to St. Paul 60 years ago from New Orleans. And it's just in the last years I've been doing some digging when I go back to New Orleans to visit a niece."

When he quit boxing and went to City Hall, Honey Boy became renowned for his easy smile, humor, gentle voice and always a "kind word for everybody."

Somewhere in those years, too, he finished Mechanics Arts High School, and studied real estate, labor law, and union administration at the University of Minnesota.

"Wife was Rebecca McCrackin. She's dead now, my daughter, too—Eloise Adams, who died in an auto accident. I have a son living near South Bend, Indiana."

Honey Boy lives alone now. "I still jump rope every day. Rope jumping is the greatest exercise there is for the muscles, the heart, the lungs."

"You'll see me on duty when they distribute all those toys at the St. Vincent de Paul Christmas toy program, too."

Honey Boy excused himself to give store directions to a family of six. They didn't know they'd been helped by a descendant of a monarch.

Keillor's the Toast of European Café Society

Paris— Tell fellow Americans you meet in Europe that you're from St. Paul and Minnesota, and you'll draw blank stares if you mention Rudy Perpich, the Twin Cities or Vikings.

But just say "Garrison Keillor" or "Lake Wobegon" or "Prairie Home Companion," and . . . .

The young woman was sitting at the next sidewalk table in Brasserie Rostan on the Boulevard St. Michel one Sunday noon. She was busy writing letters, heard us talking in English and asked if we were Americans.

We said we were, and she told us she was from Duke University, was working on her doctorate, and had been in France for two years.

"We're from St. Paul," we said.

"You are?" she said excitedly. "Then you must know the Garrison Keillor 'Prairie Home Companion' show. That's my biggest link with home. I have tapes and albums. You know, right now I'm writing a letter to the 'Prairie Home' show, telling Garrison to announce to all my friends that I'm coming home in a month, bringing 71 kilos of books. I keep in touch with home with the 'Prairie Home Companion' show on tapes and albums," she said.

It was a few nights later. We were dining in a restaurant in the Latin Quarter, and two American couples sat across from us.

Finally, one of the men leaned over to ask about some dish we had ordered.

He introduced himself as an orthodontist from Connecticut, and we told him we were from St. Paul.

"Hey," he almost shouted. "These people come from where the Garrison Keillor 'Prairie Home Companion' show is produced. We listen every Saturday night. Say, is there really a town called Lake Wobegon?"

Our conversation carried out into the street later that evening. Thanks to Keillor.

We were eating an early supper in the Café de la Paix, en route to the Paris Opera across the street.

A man sat down at the next table and ordered a shrimp cocktail and a half bottle of white wine.

He was having trouble with the menu, though, and we offered to help translate the French.

He thanked us kindly and said, "I'm a lawyer from Nashville, Tennessee. Here for the trial lawyers convention. Where you folks from?"

We told him.

"St. Paul? That's the home of the 'Prairie Home Companion' show. That's one of my wife's and my favorites. We love his country music segments and the news from Lake Wobegon. Honestly. It's a pleasure to meet somebody from St. Paul who also listens."

That started a warm, friendly 10-minute conversation on Nashville's music center, country and western music, the Grand Ole Opry and also the symphony.

The scene shifts to Vienna. We are eating dinner at a sidewalk café near the Staatsoper. A young man across the way is having trouble with the menu in German. We come to his rescue.

"Oh," he said. "You're from America, too. I'm a student, just finishing a seminar in Prague. I'm majoring in literature and my mother is a student coming from Switzerland, and we're going to meet here.

"Say, you're from St. Paul. That's the home of my favorite radio show, the 'Prairie Home Companion.' Garrison Keillor. We never miss it back home."

That introduction spawned a conversation that continued until we had finished our meal.

All of these people were curious and excited about the "Prairie Home Companion" show. They wanted to know how remodeling of the World Theater was getting along. They wondered whether there really was a Lake Wobegon town. Or whether some of those characters in the news from Lake Wobegon were real people Keillor knew.

But best of all, I guess, was the fact that Keiller was a real icebreaker who changed strangers into friends, if only for a time, in unlikely places and corners of Europe.

And if it had not been for Keillor and the "Prairie Home Companion" show, we wouldn't have found out that the young woman from Duke hasn't been home in two years and that her folks came to visit her once, or that she had an apartment near the Sorbonne, but spends most of her time in Normandy and Brittany researching in libraries and with people she meets, or that she is hoping to teach French history some day.

We wouldn't have found out that the young man who had been in Prague had found the city shabby and disappointing, but the music great, and that he was sort of at odds with life.

The orthodontist from New England and his group exchanged names of plays and cafés with us, and he and my wife had a long chat about braces on teeth.

I discovered the Nashville attorney had been a lawyer for 30 years, his wife was on the board of the Nashville symphony, and there is a lot of culture in Nashville besides country music.

Over all of our conversations hung the unseen presence of the fellow who brought us together, a man whom I have never met but, as the lawyer said, "someone you feel you've known all your life." Garrison, you helped make our European adventure more fun.

Déjà vu Surrounds Neiman's Latest Art

This is a story of déjà vu so uncanny that it raises goose bumps.

It takes place in New York City—10 years ago and just the other night—in a residential hotel called Des Artistes, in the studio of St. Paul-born artist LeRoy Neiman.

In May, 1975, a half dozen of us flew to New York City for the first look at Neiman's painting, "Baghdad on the Prairie," which he did for the city of St. Paul and Ramsey county for the 1976 Bicentennial.

We were part of the Chamber of Commerce Culture and Arts Task Force. Our leader was the chamber's Brent Baskfield, now vice president for in-flight services at Northwest Airlines.

As we walked into Neiman's studio, there he was wearing white coveralls; his wife, Janet, was there to greet us.

There, on an easel, was the painting. Brent drew the cloth cover away to applause and praise.

The drama of being there at that moment didn't escape us.

I can't remember all of the people in the group. Task force chairman John Mason of Norwest Bank was one; Wilbur Bush, executive vice president of Burlington Northern, was another.

Malcolm "Max" Lein, director of the Minnesota Museum of Art, was there. Neiman had promised to give the painting to the museum for its permanent collection. In addition, it was agreed that Neiman would offer 125 signed prints for public sale at $200 apiece and an unlimited number for $5 to $10.

To celebrate the occasion, we all adjourned to the Café des Artistes on the ground floor.

The date changes, but not the setting.

It is a Friday night a few weeks ago in New York City. We are having dinner in the Café des Artistes, which is our favorite stop when we go to New York, because of that first lunch.

As we wait for our first course, I see a familiar figure threading his way down the aisle between the tables.

It's Brent Baskfield.

"I don't believe it," we both said in unison.

Brent was with his wife, Florence, and Dr. Jay Lee and his wife Susie, and their son, David, an MIT student.

"We're on our way to see LeRoy and Janet Neiman," said Brent.

We had intended to call Neiman to say hello.

But a few minutes later, he was on the phone.

"Hey, come on up. I've got something to show you. A big surprise."

We walked into the big high-ceilinged studio.

There, on the same easel as the Bicentennial painting, was the almost-finished St. Paul Winter Carnival painting Neiman is doing for the Carnival's 1986 Centennial.

"You and Brent are the first to see it," Neiman said.

The same words he used that May morning in 1975.

There stood Baskfield, where he had stood 10 years before.

There was Neiman's wife, Janet, looking at us a little apprehensively, as she had looked at the committee a decade before.

"Déjà vu," said Neiman, who was wearing a white coverall smock.

"It's so uncanny I don't know how to explain this moment," he said.

Baskfield and I both knew Neiman had been commissioned to do the Carnival Centennial painting. He had done all his sketching when he was in St. Paul in February for the Carnival.

Just as he used the State Capitol's golden horses as his focus and the city skyline in the background in his earlier picture, so he has used his version of the first Carnival ice palace of 1886.

And woven into the foreground and background are all of the pageantry, the events spanning a century, from the first marchers to the Vulcans in their fire truck.

"I don't think I have forgotten anything or anybody or any event," he said.

He hasn't.

It's a kaleidoscope of the Carnival passing by. It moves.

On May 6, Neiman and his wife will present the painting to St. Paul to present to the Carnival people, who will purchase it for an undisclosed amount.

It Was Good to Be Part of Mama Coronado's Family

Her real name was Maria Elvira Clafira Martinez Navarro Gomez Coronado. But she only spelled it once for me. Because from that first time, she was always Mama Coronado to me.

It was only apropos that Bill Greer was the one who called to say Mama Coronado had died. It was Bill, former *Pioneer Press* city and managing editor, who introduced me to the wonderful world of Mama Coronado's cooking almost 40 years ago.

The place was at the corner of Eva and Fairfield, just across the street from the Mission of Our Lady of Guadalupe. Two tables were thick with aromas of chile powder, garlic, chile peppers, simmering meats, the enchiladas, tostadas, tamales, the arroz con pollo, sometimes chicken mole, often the chorizo sausage.

Mama Coronado by Julie Hiebert

There were eight guests plus Mama, Arturo, Jr. and Sr., Rosa, Rita, Carmen, Vera, Aurora and Gloria. Sometimes there was more cooking for family than for paying customers. But not often. Not with missionaries for Mexican food like Greer and his wife, Marion, and John and Jeanne Fisher.

Maybe it was in the fall of 1946 that I was introduced to and absorbed into the world of Mama Coronado. You were never anything but family after the first visit. For all the rest of almost 40 years, whenever we met Mama or the girls, we were treated like family, with the appropriate hugs and kisses and special foods Mama or Rosa knew we liked so much.

Once when we came back from Europe and Mama was the queen of her restaurant over on Sixth Street in Minneapolis, we said we had enjoyed paella in Spain.

A week later, Mama called. She had it for us. Then she put together something called veal Milanesa.

That first time in 1946 was almost my initiation into the realm of Mexican cooking. I couldn't have had a better tutor.

Nor could the hundreds of people who found their way to that tiny place—Spanish students, travelers who had been to South America, Mexico, Spain. They would come to dine and then go to the Spanish-language movies at the New Ray theater.

The rich and the famous came to her little café and because the strongest thing she sold was her own hot sauce for the taco chips, you brought your own beer or wine to put out imagined fires.

If there is one thing Mama disclaimed, it was the idea that Mexican food is hot. Ninety percent of her menu was as lacking in fire as any other cooking. If you wanted hot flavor, she had it. But she didn't flaunt it.

A lot of rich and famous people came to that abode on the Old West Side Flats—mayors, bank presidents, judges, students of cooking. One of her special friends was U.S. District Court Judge Miles Lord. The late Hubert Humphrey was another.

Mama taught them the pleasures of good and real and authentic Mexican cooking as she had learned it in her native state of San Luis Potosi. She never compromised, not even when the competition from new Mexican restaurants—the franchises—arrived.

"Mine is the real Mexican cooking," she said, drawing herself up to her full 5-foot-plus height.

One of the saddest days was in 1960 when urban renewal forced La Casa Coronado out of its home and over to Minneapolis. She and Arturo wanted so badly to stay in St. Paul, but there was no room for her inn.

For me, something was lost when La Casa Coronado left 189 E. Fairfield Avenue. But we stayed fairly close, even when it meant driving to Minneapolis.

Mama imported mariachi bands and Mexican entertainment. Arturo Sr. stood behind the counter and Arturo Jr. became a sort of business manager.

But there was no arguing that the person in charge, who gave the orders and who directed the kitchen staff—mostly her daughters—like a symphony, was Mama Coronado.

We shared her grief and pleasures—the day Arturo Jr. died suddenly, and the times when Arturo Sr. nearly died, then lost his eye sight. But she always came to the major food events, the major Mexican festivals and feast days with Arturo on her arm. They were very much in love.

The last time I saw Mama was on Christmas Eve a year ago at Our Lady of Guadalupe. I had taken my whole family there for midnight Mass and she was there with hers. At the end we all linked arms and sang a poignant, plaintive, but beautiful Mexican Christmas hymn.

"Isn't it wonderful how friends can meet like this and share these happy times?" she said.

Author Katkov Finds He Can't Come "Home" Again

He remembers when they used to sit on the copy desk in the *Minnesota Daily* newspaper office and dream about the future—he and Tom ("Mr. Roberts") Heggen, Harry Reasoner, Bud Nye, and Max Shulman.

His neighborhoods were the old West Side Flats, the 13th Street district and Ashland Avenue near the old Jewish Community Center on Holly Avenue.

His streets were the Loop and Grand Avenue Hill, Seven Corners and Seventh and Wabasha.

His subjects were the little people who made the human-interest stories in the night in the city. Once when he was walking home from the *Pioneer Press* newsroom at 2 a.m. he helped a cat give birth to some kittens in a gutter and after he found them a home, wrote a story that earned him his first byline.

Then he left the city for New York's newspaper city rooms and vaster human interest. He began to write fiction and books—the biography of Fanny Brice and short stories for *Colliers* magazine.

His life on West 83rd Street and down in the Village gave him grist for TV scripts for "Studio One," "Playhouse 90," "Ben Casey," "Kraft Theater," "Rawhide," and "Bonanza."

The other day Norman Katkov came home again for the first time in 32 years to the city that gave him the plots for his best-selling novel, *Eagle at My Eyes.* He came home to walk the streets of a city he no longer remembers, to look for old neighborhoods that no longer exist. He came home in triumph to autograph and talk about his fourth book—a novel, *Blood and Orchid,* based on the infamous Massie murder case in Hawaii back in the 1950s. But it was more a sentimental journey.

It was a moving experience when Norm walked into the Jewish Community Center on St. Paul Avenue to see again people he hadn't seen in three decades. The big auditorium where he spoke and autographed his book was filled with a babble of memories, awash with tears and laughter. The Friends of the St. Paul Public Library people, who arranged his visit, stood in the shadows and smiled and brushed away their own tears.

"I was scared to death about the whole thing—the deal at B. Dalton in Minneapolis and at the Center. I didn't know how I would act," Norm told me.

We sat talking for part of one morning in the lobby of the St. Paul Hotel. Later, he was invited to lunch in the Minnesota Club—"both places I would never have gone in when I worked on the paper or was growing up in the ghettos," Norm said.

"Do you know, once I would come here to Rice Park and sit and look at that club and wonder what it was like inside?"

He spoke, and I followed him through the city he no longer recognizes.

"Where is the Ryan Hotel? And the Frederic Hotel? What happened to the West Side Flats? Neighborhood House and Our Lady of Guadalupe Mission, Goldberg's market and Lafayette School and Crowley? I went there and looked for Mintz's shoe store and Kessel's bakery. All gone. There is nothing left. As if it never existed. Any of it."

"I went to find the old 13th Street neighborhood and McCall's drug store in the Portland block, where he made that wonderful hair lotion. All gone. You know what's there? A lot of freeways and ramps and a hospital?"

Norman went to the Jewish Community Center and buttonholed his friends and asked where it all was and they said, "Norman, it's all gone. This is progress."

"Do you know," said Norman, "I found two things—one of the houses where I lived at 130 E. Colorado and the house where we lived at 902 Ashland Avenue. I went to Humboldt High, where I graduated and looked for Claire McMann, whom I loved as a principal, and they told me he is dead. And Constance Currie at Neighborhood House. She's dead, too. A long time now."

He went to Ninth and St. Peter, and old Mother Merrill's was empty. So he went across the street and ate a cheeseburger with onions and pickle at Mickey's Diner. It was the same lunch he used to eat at 2 a.m. after a night on the police beat and he'd meet his friend Bill Greer, the city editor, who gave him his big chance to be a reporter.

He Put Handles on Bags, Made Shopping a Spree

I was on Seventh Place near Minnesota Street. A woman was carrying a shopping bag with handles, and I thought suddenly of Walter and Lydia Deubener.

I'm sure that the shopper had no idea that the bag was born not far from there on Seventh Street. In fact, few folks carting away big handled shopping bags from a supermarket realize that the very essence of the supermarket began with Walter and Lydia in an unpretentious grocery concession of a dime store on the north side of Seventh, about where the new World Trade Center is rising.

It was 1918. Walter had come to St. Paul from the East and married Lydia. They had met in that store, where she operated the cash-and-carry department on the balcony.

Walter noticed that shoppers were having trouble carrying large quantities of groceries because the sacks were small and poorly constructed.

"I reasoned that if somehow a large, easy-to-carry bag were invented, sales would increase and so would the ease of carrying," he once told me.

He contemplated this idea, and then decided that what was needed were deep, sturdy shopping bags with handles.

The result of trial and error through long hours at home netted a handle, fastened to sturdy string, looped under the bag. Walter and Lydia made 25, and Lydia tested them. They were perfect. Lydia pasted pictures of birds and animals and landscapes from magazines on the sides. Walter sold them for a dime.

When the Deubeners filed for a patent, they didn't know that their success was in the bag.

Business was astounding. There were never enough bags. Walter hired some girls to make them in the store basement; sales grew like mushrooms on a humid day. The basement factory moved into a storeroom on Seventh.

Stores all over America and Canada began clamoring for the Deubener shopping bag. A firm in Philadelphia manufactured a bag-making machine, and Walter moved his factory to Indianapolis, "because it was more centrally located and the shipping rates were right."

In 1919 they sold a million shopping bags.

"Then I lost count," Walter said.

Call it coincidence, but as sales of paper bags with handles improved, so did sales of merchandise. Something called the supermarket appeared on the American scene.

The late Dick Lilly, prominent St. Paul banker, told Walter that he and Lydia had done almost as much for the American economy as Henry Ford, because while nobody could break Walter's patent, adaptations of paper bags with handles are part of the Western world's way of life.

When, in the 1930s Walter sold his bag business for more than $1 million, he and Lydia turned their attention and fortune to real estate and helping other people.

One of their properties, Deubener apartments, just off St. Clair Avenue, also was on a street called Deubener Place.

Lydia stayed in the background while Walter became one of the city's most colorful personalities, one of its most compassionate to "those who were willing to work to get ahead." He gave away thousands of dollars to causes and people in dire need, but only if he thought they were the victims of fate and not their own slothfulness.

They shared their wealth without notoriety or publicity.

Walter also was one of the most vocal, demonstrative pioneers against smoking. Alcohol was equally abhorrent to him.

Along with such perks as samples of perfume, candy bars, straight-edged razors and silver dollars, he handed out his business cards which read: "No Stink Weed; No Fire Water."

His anti-smoking campaign was unflagging. When he'd park his car in a Fifth Street lot every morning and start loping down the street, frayed briefcase in hand, the word would go out through executive suites, banks, stores and brokerage houses: "Walter's on the street, put out your cigarettes."

Once, I saw him take a cigarette out of a bank president's mouth. The latter was too embarrassed to complain. Besides, Walter was a major depositor.

His fetish for exercise and fitness paralleled his feelings about tobacco and alcohol. He swam, steamed and jogged daily at the Athletic Club.

A voracious reader, he liked to say, "I've gone through a lot of literature in my life, but I've never found anything better than the Ten Commandments!"

Then, in 1937, he and Lydia began searching for their own little refuge—a place away from the tensions, noise and turmoil of life. They bought Deep in the Pines, acreage on Lake George near Itasca State Park. There they built a spacious log lodge and some cabins, where they invited their friends to spend a few days or weeks.

But for most of their summers, Walter and Lydia's best friends were animals of the forest. In 1971, some years before Lydia's death at age 87 and Walter's at age 95, they gave Deep in the Pines to handicapped people, and it became Camp Courage of the North.

Walter Deubener, as his friend Calvin Hunt said, "truly had the world by a string." And he helped all of us get a better handle on living.

They ought to put a plaque dedicated to Walter and the shopping bag with handles on the World Trade Center.

Colonel in Command of Opera Group

Fred Adelman doesn't walk. He darts. He moves as if he were triggered by springs. He speaks fast and with feeling. He is 61, a retired Air Force colonel with a long command and combat record, a retired University of Minnesota professor of meteorology and aerospace safety. He pioneered the university's program to provide rural Minnesota with physicians.

So, what's he doing at 2 p.m. on a Monday in the auditorium of Humboldt High School, watching and listening to a dress rehearsal of Opera St. Paul's "Amahl and the Night Visitors?"

Simple. Fred is also a former violin virtuoso, whose avocation is opera, and he's just been made president of Opera St. Paul.

"I figure on being a working president and I'm out here checking on the product we're selling the public," he says.

Up on the stage, the cast was getting ready for five performances for 3,000 students, but the big visibility comes this weekend at Central Presbyterian Church, where performances are at 8 p.m. Friday and 2 p.m. Saturday.

"This is what we can do really well—things like 'Amahl' and what we're planning for 1984: 'Happy Birthday, Rossini'—Gemi Beni of New York is writing that one," says Fred in a staccato voice with gestures. "Then we've got Domenico Cimarosa's 'Secret Marriage' on tap and 'Tartuffe,' paying tribute to the Moliere Year. I mean we're right on top of the situation.

"Hey, this isn't the 'other opera company' in town. This is Opera St. Paul. We're alone, in the black. We've been taking potluck at theaters around town, but, believe me, we're expecting to be at Ordway Music Theater—in big type.

"Say, we get along with Minnesota Opera just fine. I'm wearing two hats. I'm a contributor and fan of that company and the Met. Let's translate this into sports jargon: Opera St. Paul is the farm team; we're a training ground. But we're professional as the devil."

Fred and I moved out into the high school lobby, to seats at cafeteria tables, amid a swirl of gymnasts rehearsing for dance and cheerleading squads.

Adelman has been "nibbling around" Opera St. Paul ever since it started four years ago.

"Bobbie, my wife, and I watched it, then got with it. I mean we're no longer a two-person band—Virginia Hardin Olson, our founder, and Irma Wachtler, PR and promotion. They need help and a little lifting of the burdens off their shoulders. So I've got big shoulders and we've got an office now at 614 Portland Avenue in the Lung Association building, opera needs a lot of lung power, so it's apropos."

The Adelmans teach an opera seminar called Opera Around Us in the University of Minnesota Campus Club. They have a huge collection of opera slides, which they show at the sound of an aria. And they get their R and R via opera tours. They are familiar faces at Santa Fe Opera season in summer, attend the Met in New York and the Chicago Lyric Opera, sometimes go on an opera orgy through Europe—Covent Garden, La Scala, Vienna Staats, and Volks Opera, Munich.

The Adelmans don't miss a potential opera trick.

"Just the other night we went to see that Spanish zarzuela Marguerite Hedges put on at O'Shaughnessy. You know, it's something we could do at Opera St. Paul maybe, a full-blown zarzuela, in English. Placido Domingo is going to do one in Los Angeles, I hear. Marguerite gave us a new dimension in operetta," Adelman said.

Adelman might have been an international musician, too, if he'd followed the violin instead of the airplane when he grew up in St. Louis.

"We had opera all around us. I grew up with music. Then World War II and airplanes seemed more realistic than violins. It was a dilemma."

Adelman had played with symphony orchestras and with big bands.

Instead, he flew P-38s in the Pacific, decided to make the Air Force a career, did the Korea and Vietnam bit and wound up with the Air ROTC at the University of Minnesota "during the fuss in the late 1960s." He decided the Twin Cities was an opera-and concert-lover's haven.

"You don't realize how much good music is played here," says Adelman.

So he took off his Air Force hat and retired in 1974 and did the same from the University a year ago. He considers his last mission at the University, helping provide young doctors to rural areas for nine months to a year or longer, about as "rewarding a finale as I could imagine."

Now, Adelman is going to have some fun reaching towards his goal as the Twin Cities' foremost opera buff.

[*Opera St. Paul now is known as the North Star Opera. Fred Adelman died in April 1999. He was 77.*]

Island Home to Stout Dream

A couple of Saturdays ago, colleague Don Boxmeyer wrote a piece about Nick and Jane Van Brunt, an adventurous couple with a joie de vivre who are building their dream home on a tiny leaf-shaped island near the eastern shore of Bald Eagle Lake.

They aren't the first people who have dreamed on that island.

The sounds they hear in the night may not always be the whispering winds in the foliage or the lapping of the water on shore, but the echoes of little boys' voices and the clatter of young feet.

They may have to share their idyllic setting with the memory of another man named William B. Stout, who once sat on that island shore and dreamed of inventing a silvery airplane, a gleaming Pullman car and a sleek teardrop automobile.

And he did them all: the Ford tri-motor airplane, the first streamlined Budd Pullman, prototypes of the Burlington Zephyr train and the Chrysler airflow automobile.

These were his dreams in the summer of 1909 when he ran Boy Island—"A Republic for Youth"—on that piece of land in the water. Stout was the "president."

He was a popular columnist for the *St. Paul Dispatch*, who wrote under the nom de plume of Jack Knife.

It was the newspaper's idea that spring to round up as many city boys as possible and take them out to Bald Eagle Lake, where "they can absorb the refreshing air, swim, go boating, live together as a community, with democratic rules and regulations."

And Stout was chosen to lead and direct their endeavors.

He was one of the Mechanic Arts High School's famous graduates and had been a student at Hamline University (He earned his way emptying wastebaskets in the women's dormitory). Then he spent two years at the University of Minnesota and was teaching manual training at Central High School when the *Dispatch* hired him to write a column for boys.

He was a natural to organize Boy Island Republic.

So one sunny June morning in 1909, the intrepid campers gathered in front of the old *Dispatch* building at Fourth and Minnesota streets and marched 12 miles out to Bald Eagle Lake, then rowed to the island. There they pitched tents and set up camp facilities.

They formed their own government, shared cooking duties, went on nature hikes, swam, learned to use boats and generally, as Stout told me long afterwards, "had the time of their lives, got brown as berries and healthy as young lions."

But this experiment in "outward bound" living was shortlived. In fact, it lasted only one summer.

But Stout's daydreams on that island grew more vivid and real.

One day when he was still on the *Dispatch*, two St. Paul brothers named George and Earl Prudden came into his office with a

model airplane they had built, according to Jack Knife's specifica-
tions.

Stout left for Detroit before World War I to make a mark in air-
craft design for the Packard Motor Co. He headed production of
the famous Liberty engine.

I met Stout once, a year before his death at 76. It was January
1955, at the side of a swimming pool in an Arizona resort near
Phoenix. He was living nearby and had come to meet a planeload
of writers and columnists who were on a junket organized by
Gordon Gilmore, former *Pioneer Press* sports editor, who was TWA
public relations vice president.

That afternoon Stout sat in a desk chair and talked about Boy
Island and "Jack Knife." He described his other inventions and
projects—the first all-passenger airline in the United States
between Detroit and Grand Rapids in 1926; the Navy Torpedo
plane; the Ford Tri-motor, of course; the Pullman all-metal car;
and the tear-drop automobile.

He was voluble about his World War II invention of a house on
a trailer with collapsible or folding walls that made it three times
the trailer size when it was assembled. Thousands of them were
sold during World War II for housing projects.

He seldom came back to his old home haunts. But in 1947 he
was invited to speak at a University of Minnesota convocation and
University of Minnesota Institute of Technology Alumni dinner.

Stout also took a sentimental journey around Bald Eagle Lake
and said he stopped to look at Boy Island, where so many of his
dreams began one summer long ago.

The Van Brunts have a greater heritage to preserve than they
know.

Retired Railway Mail Clerk Delivers Memories

Don Rohrer dropped in the other day and we rode a train of thought through a profession with a past that is almost forgotten in this modern day of jet transportation.

Once, we rode through the cold and dust and excitement of a gloomy December day in the railway mail car of the old Milwaukee Hiawatha, hurtling, rattling, shaking east towards Santa Claus, Ind. I was writing about carrying tons of letters to Santa.

Another time, Rohrer also bid me farewell on a steamy summer morning in the Union Depot as I spent a day and most of a night riding a mail car on the old Great Northern Western Star to Fargo, North Dakota. With me were such luminaries among the railway mail clerks as Orrin Root and Ed Rauen.

I didn't know it then, but I was writing about the end of an era of romance and speed that began when the first mail pouch was put aboard a mail train in 1864 and ended for Rohrer and the fraternity of railroad mail clerks Sept. 18, 1970.

That was the night the Milwaukee Fast Mail No. 56, nicknamed the Chic 'n' Min line, pulled out of St. Paul Union Depot for Chicago with the last mail train.

In the halcyon days of the RMS (Railway Mail Service) and the RPOs (Railway Postal cars), Rohrer estimates 600 clerks rode 100 trains through the St. Paul depot each day.

They fought time and speed, weather and weaving tracks. Their coordination of body and mind was unchallenged, if largely unsung, by a public that really never knew they existed, who never understood that the letter from home, the check in the mail, the birthday or Christmas package would never have arrived if it hadn't been for men like Don Rohrer.

Fewer than 200 former clerks are left and fewer than that turn out for the annual reunion dinners, where they feast on memories. Rohrer is their historian.

"I am collecting as many stories from the survivors as I can and writing a few myself," said Rohrer, who has contributed tales of the rails to national magazines and has begun (but abandoned) a book about railway mail service.

There was an esprit de corps the Marines could have envied about those men as I recall them myself, on those runs I made. The pride in their profession was incredible.

Their nemesis and victories came from those long mechanical arms on station platforms that caught and exchanged mail pouches on the fly.

On trains such as the Great Northern's Empire Builder, Rohrer said, with only one stop between Minneapolis and Fargo, the clerk had to leave his sorting bin 31 times to dispatch and collect those pouches as the train swept past the hooking arm at 80 mph.

"Then he'd have to quickly open the sacks to sort out the mail that might have been destined for the next town, maybe six miles away, get it into the right pouch and back out the door on the metal arm five minutes later," he said.

"I'll never forget one of my first runs. I was subbing on the Soo Line and working each town on the fly," Rohrer said. "I kept missing the pouches waiting to be caught. I got more discouraged every town."

"Finally, at one stop, I got out to pick the mail up out of the platform side mail box. The engineer leaned out and said, 'Sorry, son, but I've got a bum flap in the cab up here and that's been knocking down all your pouches.' I felt as if I'd been liberated from purgatory," Rohrer said.

Working the fast trains, the crews often used landmarks en route to gauge when the next station would appear and they'd work the mechanical arm.

"But it was impossible on night runs and even sometimes during the day. We had a red barn near some town in Wisconsin that we always used as a marker. One day we ran by that town and I couldn't figure out why. Next time I discovered they'd painted the red barn gray."

Every depot had its "depot dog" and the mail crews used to watch the dogs compete for the pouches with the agents when they'd drop the sacks on the platform.

"I'll never forget one dog. He'd grab that pouch and start down the platform, trailing letters and magazines, with the entire depot staff running after him," Rohrer said.

Like the crews who worked them, the railway mail cars have almost disappeared. Minnesotans still get a glimpse of how it was on old Northern Pacific Railway mail-sorter car No. 1102, refurbished and used by the Minnesota Transportation Museum.

"I guess modern methods are better than human hands," Rohrer said. "But one thing a computer or automatic sorter can never do. Not even a jetliner."

"It can never provide a thrill for a small boy standing on a lonely station platform in a small town, watching the fast mail thunder by, waving to the mail clerk who catches and dispatches a pouch with a blurring click of the mechanical arm. And getting the candy bar hurled at his feet and a salute as the train's observation car disappears up the track."

Bittersweet Love Story Staged at Old TB Pavilion

The other noon, I crossed paths with Jim Griffin, retired deputy police chief, whose 42 years in uniform span my life at the *Dispatch.* When we had finished remembering old friends and faces around the Loop, we came at last to Willard Vinitsky, the newsie who turned his stand at Seventh and Wabasha into the city's crossroads of gossip and conversation.

But we talked of another of his roles.

Willard and his wife, Doris, lived a touching and tragic love story. She was an appealing girl, whom he wooed and won sometime during his few hours away from the job hawking papers.

Their marriage in the early 1940s was idyllic.

You would never have guessed looking at him.

In his working attire—Jackie Coogan-style wool cap, bulky ink-stained leather jacket, baggy trousers and scuffed boots—Willard was a Damon Runyon character like his colleagues. When you bought a paper from Willard, you got that and all the latest inside information on sports, politics and crime. And also the news about Doris and later, daughter Karen.

Willard brought Doris a house on Ashland Avenue, and some days he worked 18 hours selling papers to pay the bills.

Then tragedy came in the guise of tuberculosis in the days when cures were still elusive. Doris went to a bed in the TB pavilion of old Ancker Hospital.

It broke Willard up. He would come into the newsroom and rub tears out of his eyes with those big ink-smudged hands and tell us about Doris and all the others lying there, day after day, dying from boredom as well as disease.

They had radio, but TV was still in the wings.

So Willard did something about it. He began to canvas all the night clubs and theaters and restaurants with entertainment, asking performers to come and put on a show for the TB patients.

The Musicians Union and American Guild of Variety Artists gave Willard their approval, and once a week he would put on his best clothes, take the streetcar to wherever there was an act or group on stage. He became a Stage Door Johnny of the most persistent type, haunting dressing rooms and talent-agent offices.

In those years, Freddie's and the Happy Hour in Minneapolis brought in the big names. So did the Radisson Flame Room and Nicollet Hotel Terrace. Nobody could turn down Willard when they heard his pitch.

He got Sophie Tucker, Cab Calloway, Satchmo, Duke Ellington, Hildegard; he got George Jessel and the Ink Spots. He got big bands and small groups. He persuaded comedians, opera singers and symphony soloists to go to Ancker Hospital once a month to give those patients the shows of their lives.

News of what Willard did began to spread across the state and nation, and word was: "When you play the Twin Cities, don't forget Willard Vinitsky's shows at the TB ward."

Willard would come into the newsroom a few days earlier and hand us a slip of paper listing the month's acts, which we dutifully published.

We also published his appeals for help to pay for the entertainers' transportation and maybe a lunch or snack. City hall politicians, officials and businessmen all chipped in; so did his friends on the police force and fire department. But nobody knew how often Willard dug into his own pocket to buy cab fare or a meal for some musician, dancer or young actor.

And all the time, in between shows, Willard walked every afternoon to visit Doris and josh the other patients. He always took roses.

Doris spent 5½ years in the ward and then went home because there was nothing more anybody thought they could do. Willard and she both knew she was dying, but she wanted those last few months in her own home. She died there in May 1951.

A relative says their daughter has lived in a Faribault institution since she was 7 or 8. Willard lived with that heartbreak, too.

But Willard didn't neglect his own special people in the TB pavilion. The shows went on as always, even after Doris died.

"I'm going to do it as a memorial to her," he told me one night when he came with the month's playbill.

Doris didn't live to know that, because of their love, the Newspaper Guild of the Twin Cities gave Willard the first public-service award for his compassion and generosity to people whom he considered much worse off than he was.

What ended those shows at Ancker wasn't his flagging interest, but television.

"You know, everybody watches TV now out there, and I can't match that talent in my package," he said.

And of course, TB was being conquered and the old pavilion emptied and finally the new St. Paul-Ramsey Hospital was built.

Willard wasn't around to see all that. He died in April 1957. He was 48. They said it was cancer that had been gnawing at him, but I believe it was really grief.

Horsemen's "Rein"—Tough Riders a Carnival Legend

On Winter Carnival parade days, they rode into town from South St. Paul like cowboys celebrating the end of a big roundup, firing their six-shooters—42 horsemen, followed by 250 marchers and their own drum corps.

You could, but you didn't dare—start a Grande or Torchlight parade without them leading it. Occasionally, they got some guest riders like then-Gov. Harold Stassen and a young lawyer named Harold LeVander, who was destined to become governor.

But the regulars were hard-riding, macho men—livestock commission agents, dealers, stockyards staff—wearing Western Stetsons and doffing workday boots caked up to the ankles with cow and sheep dung for spiffy dress boots.

In those rollicking post-parade sessions, they rode their horses on Wabasha and Robert and down Fifth, reining in along the bar at the old Covered Wagon—well, maybe one or two horses—and the rest wearing spurs that jingled and jangled.

They maneuvered a horse into the St. Paul Hotel lobby one night, and their leader, John Marthaler, performed a historic feat in the old Ryan Hotel back bar after one Torchlight parade when he rode his horse the length of the bar, ordered drinks for everybody and "one water for my horse because he's driving."

They called themselves the South St. Paul Hook-em-Cow Riders, and their antics and showmanship at Carnivals for more than 20 years created legends, as well as lore—true tales embellished only by time.

They are credited with inspiring an immortal phrase uttered by a St. Paul Public Works sanitation crew man following behind the 1939 Grande Parade: "If you had my job, you wouldn't call this a one-horse town."

Their long "rein" ended in 1956, although they did an encore in 1960.

But their exploits and adventures persist in horse yarns as Carnival Week nears. They gather in the lobby of the Livestock Exchange Building in the afternoon to upstage each other until one of the secretaries chases them upstairs into the conference room where I found the "Old Saddle Club" assembled one afternoon last week.

Only a cadre are left of that once noble and courageous troop of riders who carried the name of South St. Paul to glory and sometimes notoriety.

Most of them are in their 70s and retired, but the aroma of the yards lures them back almost every day with a nostalgic scent. They are: Charley Neren, 70, their "mouthpiece," a half-century veteran in the yards "who just can't stay away"; Art Shanahan, the "old man" at 80, who rode through the whole era; Howard Johnson, 71, a 52-year veteran of the yards; Jim Kelleher, 68, still in the yards; Art Carlson, 64, a 40-year man with huge joie de vivre; Darrell Iliff, 56, who still puts in a day weighing cattle; and Henry Wertheimer Jr., 58, whose father, Henry Sr., achieved lasting fame buying and selling in the old turreted Livestock Exchange Building.

That afternoon, primed by a few cups of coffee—"In the old days we wouldn't have touched anything that didn't come out of a bottle," says Charley—they "saddled up and rode" through a picturesque era.

It was the time of carnivals and years when there were 28 commission firms and 27 dealers at the stockyards, when Swift, Cudahy and Armour were at a peak and the horse barns never had any less than 600 animals, when the Hook-em-Cows could choose from 100 of the best horses.

"What kind of horses did we ride? Just saddle horses. That wasn't the time of quarter horses and Arabians. Every man in the yards had his own he rode on the job," says Art Shanahan.

"And at Carnival time, we'd all pick out the ones we wanted and use them. The most remarkable thing was that these horses spent most of their time in the yards; they never were exposed to crowds and noise and cars and guns firing blanks in their ears. But do you know, we never had an incident, not with a horse. With the riders, there were plenty, but never a horse," says Art Carlson.

"We got our name and tradition from Charley Govern way back in 1916," says Shanahan. "Then John Marthaler revived us when the Carnival revived in the 1930s. But we'd been riding in rodeos and festivals all over Minnesota."

"We weren't exactly a drinking bunch, but every saloon was a desert after we left," says Charley.

"One night somebody shot the stockings off two waitresses. They got a little hostile until we gave them each $20 for new socks," says Carlson.

"Well, of course, we never rode our horses home in the dark after a parade and, actually, only a few tried to take their horses pub-trotting," Charley says. "Mostly, we kept them down behind the old FOK (Farwell, Ozmun Kirk) building on Second Street," says Iliff.

The riders would book hotel rooms for the night. One morning, a rider who wishes to remain anonymous, woke up with an excruciating pain in his back. He called an ambulance. He figured he'd fallen someplace and broken his back. When they came to lift him out of his bed, they found he'd slept all night on his spurs.

The voices stop suddenly. They look around at each other.

Then Shanahan says, "I lived my day riding and roping and landing in the dust after a rough ride. We were a great bunch for

50 years, one for all and all for one; we had courage and were rough and tough and we added fun and frolic wherever we rode to perform and play."

"It's been said of a rider, 'When one gets bucked off, you hit the ground hard and don't bounce back . . . that's the time to quit.' That's what I did."

He spoke for most of those in the room.

The Colonel Is a Lady—and Haven for Hundreds

When night falls on the city, the dim, little lamps are lit in perhaps hundreds of rooms across the near-Loop and fringe areas.

Here, in rooming houses, live the "oldsters," those men and women past 65, who have no homes of their own and thin family ties. So thin that they live alone.

And the hub of their universe is a big, brick building, cool inside on a hot summer day, a place where the rocking chairs look inviting and there is always the makings of one more sandwich in the kitchen refrigerator upstairs.

This is Volunteers of America hall at 349 Washington, looking out over Rice Park, which Lt. Col. Nina A. Forsmoe, executive secretary, calls the "gallery."

Because, if you take a stroll in Rice Park on a sunshiny morning, quite a few of Col. Forsmoe's best customers will be sitting there, nodding or reading or just resting.

And now meet the colonel. Because the story of the St. Paul branch of the Volunteers of America, financed by public contributions, has been her story, too, since 1926.

And you get the right perspective if you look at it through her eyes.

To clear up the military title. There is really nothing military about it at all, says Miss Forsmoe.

"It's just a way we have in the Volunteers of designating length of service." And Miss Forsmoe probably will be remembered longer as Maj. Forsmoe, as was the case with her beloved predecessor, Maj. Martha L. Starr.

What brought Col. Forsmoe to the Volunteers as an employee is the same thing that brings many of those who sit on the other side of her desk—personal problems.

"I had lost my father and mother within 14 months and I had the feeling I wanted to get away and start something new," she said.

"And so I came here to work and I am still here."

Maj. Starr, when she signed up Col. Forsmoe, said: "There is one thing about our work. No two days are alike." And they never have been, says Miss Forsmoe.

The "oldsters," as she calls them, make it like that. It is they who use the hall the most, although as an emergency assistance agency and haven for the distressed, the Volunteers also see hundreds of mothers, widowed with families, or those whose husbands earn so little they cannot provide some of the social recreation any family needs.

For these mothers and their children the Volunteers each summer provide a week's camping, all free, at Clear Lake at Forest Lake.

This year 500 to 600 mothers and children—and also some of the oldsters—took their turn at the Clear Lake "resort."

But this began with the oldsters and their stereotyped, little rooms, with the fading wallpaper, the iron beds, the closets and a calendar hanging on the wall.

The Volunteers is for them.

It is for men like Bill, a pensioner, who has been twice slugged and robbed during the past few months.

"The last time he was almost killed," says Miss Forsmoe. "So I sent his bloody clothes to the laundry and Bill got out to the camp for a few days to rest in the sun."

The Volunteers is for the little old ladies who cannot entertain their guests in their drab rooms, so they will go up to the kitchen, cook a meal, set the table, complete with flowers, and entertain their friends as if they were home.

The Volunteers is for Fred, who plays the mouth organ, and Millie, who wants to sing and is allowed to sing to her heart's content, although, as Miss Forsmoe says, "It is not because of her lovely voice."

Most of these oldsters belong to the Sunset club, which meets for lunch on the third Wednesday every month.

And while Miss Forsmoe may not see all of them the rest of the year, they come back like waifs out of the storm during the Thanksgiving-Christmas season. The annual Volunteers of America Thanksgiving dinner is one of the institutions around the city now.

From noon until night on that day, maybe 400 men and women will show up to eat the meal that is served. Then they will adjourn to their checker games or tend to their knitting, renewing old friendships.

In the long, graying line of those who pass by Miss Forsmoe's door are many just finished serving prison sentences.

Two stories will tell about them:

The gray-haired man of high intelligence who, suddenly after 15 or 20 years, found himself free.

Thirty-six hours later he was crying into his hands at Miss Forsmoe's desk.

"I've been away from it all so long I can't face the outside world anymore," he said.

"But he learned to face it," she says, "little by little."

And then there was the second man.

He came from upstate and had been sentenced to a long term because, during a burglary, a policeman had been killed.

Miss Forsmoe heard about him and his story, like a broken record, that he was not guilty.

"Whether he was or wasn't is something I can't say," says she.

"But after awhile, he became ill. And I visited him once a month for years, watching him grow from a young man into an old man."

And at length, Miss Forsmoe was able to shorten his sentence and he was released.

"We brought him over from the beautiful St. Croix valley to the city he hadn't seen in 30 years," she said.

"And the first morning he was here, he walked out on the veranda and stood looking at the park. And I wonder what went through his mind as he saw the cars, the people, the buildings."

Watching him there may have brought some satisfaction to Miss Forsmoe, who had worked so long to give him just a little freedom. (He died in St. Louis a few years later.)

It was, I suppose, the kind of a gesture you would expect from an organization whose motto is:

"Live and Let Live."

[*The Volunteers of America building is long gone, replaced by the Ordway Music Theatre.*]

Getting There and Back

Memories on Board During Recent Visit to Depot

On one of the last days of this year, I trudged down Fourth Street through the gray snow to Union Depot Place, and the old echoes and events came flooding down the heavy granite steps to meet me.

With mixed emotions, I had gone to see what is and will be and to remember what had been there, to keep my own communion with the past before embarking on the new, flavorful, busy adventure.

I glanced at the sharp edges of the steps and relived a summer's night in 1959 when I was about to board the Great Northern Empire Builder for Seattle. My youngest daughter, Polly, fell and cut open her head on one of those steps. And amid the bleeding and anxiety in stationmaster Eddie Bruer's office, a GN public relations man Charles "Dinty" Moore managed to get me into my roomette, and all along the way, he sent updates on Polly's recovery.

I thought of a happier occasion on those same steps when the late Joseph L. Shiely Sr., the concrete-sand-cement man, took all of his grandchildren and their friends, including my two daughters, to the Seattle World's Fair in 1962. He posed all of them on the depot steps for pictures.

I wasn't even through the doors and I was already chasing the bittersweet past when the depot was for trains.

My table on the Signals restaurant platform was close to the spot where the bands had met the St. Paul sailors who had come off the destroyer *Ward* one night in January 1942. The men were coming home after firing the first shot at Pearl Harbor. By the time they got to the front concourse-lobby they were enveloped by cheers, screams, laughter and tears. One sailor, I recall, ran outside and gleefully rolled in the snow.

From my vantage point, I recalled seeing Bill Hutson, the day stationmaster, and Burlington's Jack Lindstad, wearing his passenger agent's cap, hurrying down the long concourse to meet the Burlington Zephyr.

On one such afternoon, in late January 1946, my new bride and I came up the long steps from Gate 19. I was home from World War II at last, and there were Bill and Jack waiting to greet me as if I had merely gone to Red Wing.

One morning in February 1942 it was bitterly cold. I was at Gate 22 with Harry Congdon, the big, smiling Union Depot general manager. We were waiting for Alexander Woollcott, author, critic and raconteur, who was coming to speak at the Women's Institute. I was going to be his manager for a day.

We waited through all the incoming Chicago trains and then, at last, after the Milwaukee Pioneer Limited arrived, we saw him— the great and portly author and lead in "The Man Who Came to Dinner," crawling up the stairs on his hands and knees. He had a bad heart and he hadn't found the elevator. It was probably the most humiliating entrance an actor ever made.

Amid the hubbub of the new Depot Place the day I was reminiscing, I listened and heard, from somewhere in the past, that stentorian voice of the taped train caller, his words a singsong in the cavernous concourse: "Your attention, please! The Omaha's Nightingale, now ready at Gate 10, for Mankato,

St. James, Windom, Worthington, Sioux City and Omaha. All aboard!"

In my mind, I rode that train again through the darkness, across the moonlit prairies of southwestern Minnesota, hearing the mournful whistle.

I recalled the announcement for the North Coast Limited, the Hiawatha, the Rock Island Rocket, the Western Star and the Mainstreeter, North Western's 400 and Burlington Blackhawk, the Omaha's North American and Soo Line's Winnipeger.

I remembered the magic of hearing my train called and the flurry of activity to get on board: the sudden shuffle of feet, the reaching for luggage, the porters wheeling big vans loaded with suitcases, the red light blinking, and the gateman escorting passengers down the long stairs to the puffing steam locomotives. Later they were throbbing diesel engines.

But one morning, when we waited for the Chicago-bound Zephyr, somebody forgot to let us know. The train came in and left without its St. Paul passengers. I will never forget the look of disbelief on the gateman's face as he watched the silver streamliner pull out and realized all of us were still upstairs.

Luckily a towerman at the Dayton's Bluff signal center got the word and the train returned for us.

Sometimes the trains were late or connections missed and then the depot restaurant and coffee shop were filled, although not quite as elegant as Gordon's nor as eclectic as Signals.

Prior to this lunch date, the last time I walked out of the station was the last day it was open and the last day a train came there. The last train was the last Burlington Zephyr and I was on it, with the late Kermit Hedman, the train-loving sheriff of Ramsey County, and his wife Eyleen.

Eddie Bruer, the last stationmaster, was at the trainside to welcome us home for the last time, and Kermit took the Burlington Zephyr train announcement board home for a souvenir.

I just took these stories.

The Friendly Peanut

For the residents whose homes border the Milwaukee's Hastings to Stillwater branch, the big event on most evenings is the run of a friendly freight, affectionately called the "Peanut."

Skirting the St. Croix for 26 miles, through a tunnel of trees on one of the railroad's historic lines, No. 301-302 performs its mission sometime between 6 p.m. and midnight.

We say "sometime" because the "Peanut" has things pretty much to itself on the line, with no competition for the right of way, save a few scared rabbits and occasionally a fox or a deer.

Generally, however, No. 301-302 leaves Hastings for Stillwater about 7 p.m., except when it goes at 6:30 p.m. or even an hour later.

It is a friendly-type train because most of the crew knows every foot of ground on the run, and the names of the people who live on either side of the track. The householders, in turn, have come to know the crew and regard the "Peanut" as a colorful part of valley life.

The train has been known in the past to stop and give a man a lift to the next town. And it has come in handy on some social occasions. There was, for instance, the first wedding anniversary of St. Paulite Don O'Grady, who, in 1946, lived at St. Croix Beach.

With no car, he and his wife celebrated one year of wedded bliss by hopping on the "Peanut," which ran then during daylight. They rode to Bayport where they spent the night in the White Pine Inn, returning via "Peanut" the next morning.

So it is that a certain camaraderie has sprung up between train and people, which is in evidence every time the rhythmic, quick-tempoed sound of the little diesel echoes off the rock cliffs of an evening.

House lights blink on and off, with an answering signal from the train crew and occasionally a bellowing blast from the whistle which gives the engine a false aura of ferociousness. Actually locomotive No. 1619 is a happy fellow.

This was apparent on the bitterly cold night when we rode train No. 301-302.

Although ostensibly the "Peanut" can carry passengers, we were the first the crew had seen in a long while and Conductor Harry Rouleau had the pot-bellied stove in the caboose stoked to red-hot heat for the occasion.

His brakeman that night was Wayne Keene and up front in No. 1619, veteran engineer Lou Dodge was at the throttle and the fireman was Dale Kryder.

It was 7:28 p.m. when Lou "hi-balled" out from behind the Hastings depot, late because he had to give way to some mainline traffic before crossing over the Burlington onto his own domain.

The manifest included 29 empties, vanguard of cars headed for the annual St. Croix ice harvest near Lakeland, and a dozen other pieces of rolling stock, earmarked for Bayport and Stillwater.

Ghosts of other years on the line walked abroad.

Here was Sheare's siding, eight miles below Afton, and next Lumber Coulee where, long ago, farmers brought their grain on wagons around a circular road to the water's edge. And the trail is still visible, even in the light of a trainman's lantern beam.

Elevator Bay loomed up dead ahead, although you couldn't distinguish it from the rest of the woods. But Engineer Dodge remembers the old elevator that stood along a siding and grain-filled wagons lined up outside in the crisp, autumn mornings.

A modern home to the right, on the water's edge, came out of the dark, looking like a Christmas tree with its colored holiday lights strung outside. The lights blinked for the train and Engineer Dodge gave an acknowledging honk and flashed his lights.

Roy H. Dose, St. Paul roofing man, who owns the house, came out to wave.

Afton was drowsing when engine 1619 hooted for the crossing, but St. Croix Beach was alight and waiting.

Residents and train crew exchanged hearty blinks and whistles. And at the Street home, alongside the track, a little boy stood in the living room window, waving a flashlight back and forth.

That's the way it went. Cut out 29 cars at Lakeland; open the gates at the Omaha main line crossover opposite Hudson; switch cars at Bayport and finally the downhill roll into Stillwater where the caboose was moved to the rear of the train.

We were up in the cab of 1619 for the return trip, with Lou and his fireman, munching on a ham sandwich and fruit cake baked by Mrs. Dodge.

It was dark in most of the houses along the way by now. And ground fog, in wisps and pockets, hung over the track as the "Peanut" curved back toward Hastings with a pulsating roar and at an outrageous speed of 15 miles an hour.

Just before midnight, the welcome signal lights on the Burlington crossover near Hastings loomed out of the fog in a blur of yellow dots.

No. 1619's bell was clanging grandly when Lou nosed her behind the Hastings depot a few minutes later.

Caboose Cookery

When the history of cooking is written, it will be less than a complete chronology if at least one chapter isn't devoted to what for want of a better name, we call "Caboose Cookery."

And it should be suggested that historians get something down on paper about it pretty soon because this fine old institution is fast fading from the right of way.

Shorter time schedules for freight trains and the appearance of roadside eating establishments have just about reduced "Caboose Cookery" to percolating a pot of coffee on the flat-top coal stove.

But in bygone years some of the best cooks in the business were trained in cabooses. And the operating offices of lines serving St. Paul are full of graduates, each of whom achieved some fame in the preparation of a mulligan stew, New England boiled dinner or rabbit pot roast, the rabbit having been caught fresh that day.

We talked to a former student of "Caboose Cookery" in our investigation and he lamented that the art is gone, except on freight trains operating over remote branch lines.

Paul Byers, general chairman of the Brotherhood of Railroad Trainmen in this area, said that in 24 years as a brakeman and conductor he put out some well-received pot roast dinners on his caboose.

"Why," he said, "I even baked biscuits."

Mr. Byers explained that the menus on cabooses generally fell in the stew class because the cook, also a crew member, had to whip up something he wouldn't have to watch all the time while it was simmering.

He'd do a little switching, hop on to check the corned beef, then go back and do some more switching.

Mr. Byers said that the cook's job was rotated, but if a man was found to have an especial forte for the task, he usually had his way. That included doing the marketing at towns along the route. The engineer was informed ahead of time where the best bargains were on sale that week and he'd give the cook plenty of time to negotiate his business with the butcher.

Domestic meat was the mainstay of "Caboose Cookery," of course, but on some lines, wild game added savory variety to the menu.

"Out on the Northern Pacific branch line between Morris and Little Falls," Mr. Byers recalled, "we'd get off and hunt awhile in season during a long stop. And we'd bag duck or pheasant."

Nothing at Maxim's was ever eaten with greater enthusiasm. When a man's been out juggling freight cars around all morning, roast pheasant is like reaching the promised land.

There was one disadvantage to having a good cook aboard a caboose, however. Trainmasters were continually coming around to inspect operations, especially at mealtime. And it would be difficult to prove, but the texture of the gravy and the consistency of the soup unquestionably had an influence on reports that went back to the home office.

The leisurely pace on some of the "one train a day" lines many years ago also permitted crews to reconnoiter farmhouses where the best cooks in the county held forth. And occasionally about noon, these trains might be unaccountably detained, by pure coincidence, of course, near a farm where hot apple pie and roast pork were ready for plates.

The Record Run

The speedometer needle flutters between 91 and 92. The mighty diesel motors capable of turning out 4,250 horsepower throb behind the wall of the tiny engine cubicle.

Whipping out on the curves behind the locomotive like a kite tail ride six cars of the silver train. The buffet coach just behind the locomotive is busy, even at 11:30 a.m.

In the diner, the steward is getting ready to send out "First call for lunch." Two youngsters romp on the carpet of the parlor car while their mother knits.

Up in the vista-domes, passengers watch the scenery; some doze in the sun; others chat with Trainman O. T. Olson of Minneapolis as he walks through the cars.

The meandering Mississippi, ice-bound, sweeps along to the left of the track; to the right are the hills beyond the valley. Chicago is less than three hours behind; St. Paul about three and a half hours ahead.

And the train, Burlington Zephyr No. 21, Chicago to the Twin Cities, hurtles en route from East Dubuque to Prairie du Chien, on the fastest scheduled run between two points of any train in the world.

The Burlington Zephyrs by Julie Hiebert

It's cozy, almost crowded in the tiny forward cab. A fan at the rear blows heat into the compartment. To the left Fireman Jerry Cymanick of La Crosse watches the signals. Clear, caution, stop? Following the letter of Rule 34, he calls out the signal setting to the "Man of the train, the hour and the ride"—the engineer.

Today he is J. C. Harmacek, also of La Crosse, whose steady left hand on the throttle, turned up to the sixth notch, controls the train and the welfare of those hundreds riding in the cars behind.

His right hand is never far from the air brake lever. Every now and then, as the Zephyr streaks down the valley, he reaches for one of two handles on the end of dual ropes.

And the horn, like the sound of a frightened animal in hurried flight, bellows and roars up and down the river.

Two longs, one short, one long. For a grade crossing.

"He yanks on only one cord. The second is a spare. In case the diaphragm on the first horn breaks."

The man who has just said that is standing behind me. J. C. Kuschel of La Crosse, road foreman, assigned to answer my questions on today's regular, record run.

Rules do not permit the engineer or fireman to talk to riders in the cab of No. 21 at 91 miles an hour.

This memorable ride in the Zephyr cab, for which small boys and big boys would give their fondest possession, began back at Savannah, Illinois, at 10:50 a.m. That is where the Zephyr makes one of its few stops, to change crews, on its hurried 437-mile run.

Even when it pauses, No. 21 is a nervous thing, eager to get away. And the timetable permits only one-minute station stops.

But we're 10 minutes late as Engineer Harmacek swings into the cab, bites off a fresh wad of chewing tobacco and looks back for Conductor E. F. Mueller's signal.

When it comes, the engineer blows four blasts on the horn to "Call in the flag," which means the flagman at the rear is to climb aboard.

A thin-sounding whistle pierces the locomotive cab. Flagman O.H. Jauch's answering report.

The engineer shifts the throttle to the first notch and the pulsing diesel motors make contact. Then he moves it to the second notch and the locomotive glides forward. For a few seconds the engines roar, then settle back to an idle as the engineer shuts off the throttle and tests his brakes.

The flagman at the rear reports again, by whistle, that the brakes on the last car are set. The brakes are released, the throttle moved forward again, this time steadily, notch by notch.

There are eight settings in the throttle, but speed restrictions seldom permit a setting beyond six. At eight the train could make 120 miles an hour.

And No. 21 rolls out of Savannah.

The next stretch, between Savannah and East Dubuque, is a warmup for the record run. But since that record is made—as routine—every day, rain, snow or shine, nobody is much impressed, except me.

No. 21 is only seven minutes late out of East Dubuque as it enters the famous part of its schedule.

"This is it," I said. And Foreman Kuschel pulls out his stop watch.

"Ordinarily," he said, "it will take 7½ miles from a standstill to reach a speed of 90 miles an hour. Let's time it now."

The powerful engines scream in high pitch as Engineer Harmacek shoves the throttle ahead. The ties on the track ahead pass under the blunt locomotive nose in a blur.

"Three miles and we're doing 75," said Kuschel.

The engineer leans out of his window and fires a quid of tobacco at the mile posts. The only relaxed thing in the cab is the engineer. But when you've been riding locomotive cabs since 1910 and taking passenger runs for about eight years, it gets to be old hat. Except that everlasting vigilance, those narrowed eyes piercing the window, watching the signals, the track, for cars coming up on the grades.

"Four and a half miles and the needle says 85." Kuschel again.

"Six miles. We've done it in six miles," he shouts above the shriek of the straining motors.

I look at the speedometer, through which passes tape that will record every mile of speed for future checking.

It hits 91, inches up to 92 and drops back to 91.

Engineer Harmacek has a limit of 94 miles an hour, which he never reaches. If he did, the emergency brakes on the train would stop it.

And as we pound and rock up the riverside I learn the secret of the Zephyr's success. Steady speed, not fits and spurts. But a steady 90-91.

If you look ahead, it's hard to imagine you're going 90 miles an hour. But open the cab window and stick out your head to watch the trailing cars and the wind slaps like a lash at your face, all but searing it.

Harmacek held it there for that ride to Prairie du Chien. And when, out of the light river haze the town appears, the train begins slowing for the station. We roll to a stop at the far end of the platform. Mr. Kuschel checks his watch.

Fifty-four and six-tenths miles, in 38 minutes. Average speed: 86.2 miles per hour.

Engineer Harmacek lit a cigarette and said he'd rather be ice fishing down on the river.

Dan Patch on Wheels

In the realm of historic Minnesota horseflesh, men still take off their hats and face the village of Savage out of respect to Dan Patch, whose pacing record of a mile in 1:55 for a long time was not matched. But there was another Dan Patch, which also made some exciting history in the field of railroading.

And though I am not as old as some people think, I count, among my fortunes, the times when, in the 1920s, I rode the old Dan Patch, that orange one-car gas electric train.

I got on board during the closing years of a short, but colorful, career of this remarkable, jolting, bucketing train which ran from Minneapolis, down through the Minnesota river valley and on south to Lakeville, Northfield, Faribault and eventually Mankato.

I once heard it ran even farther, south of Mankato, but this was always a vague detail.

In my day, Dan Patch belonged to the Minneapolis, Northfield & Southern railway. But in the beginning, it ran under the direction of the Minneapolis, St. Paul, Rochester and Dubuque Electric Traction Co.

Dan Patch, on wheels, had a close liaison with Dan Patch, the horse. Both were owned and promoted by Colonel M. W. Savage. And, at one point, the Dan Patch rail line skirted the old track at Savage, Minnesota, where the famous horse lived.

But beyond that there is little similarity. Dan Patch, the train, never set any speed records. Its claim to history is mainly because, as Colonel Savage wrote to the stockholders: "It was the first gas electric railroad in the world."

And, in its very existence, the Dan Patch line left villages and prosperous farms in the wake of the right of way.

It created at least one fabulous place of fun and frolic, Antler's Park on Prairie Lake, still a suburban residential hideaway for Twin Citians.

But no longer is it the gay resort it once was, except in the memories of those who went there in the long ago.

All this began on July 4, 1910. The train ran that day. Not just one Dan Patch, but several, from 54th and Nicollet to Antler's Park.

Rose Anne Hanft of 194 W. Congress has written an excellent description of those outings at Antler's Park:

"Whole families would make this trip, and for the children, it was the big event of the summer. They would arrive at 54th and Nicollet early if they wanted a seat. At 11 a.m. a Dan Patch train pulled out of the terminal and headed south through the beautiful hilly country, past the many small stations named for the farmers whose lands the tracks cut through, past the Auto club, the Savage farm and finally reached Antler's Park.

"The college groups usually went to the attractive pavilion. In one end of it, there was an ice cream parlor where sodas, sundaes, pop, but no liquor, were sold. The rest of the pavilion was a dance floor. Beautiful chandeliers hung from the ceiling, murals decorated the walls, and the floor was made of exceptionally fine wood. The open side of the dance floor had a vine-covered walk. . . . Dances were 10 cents for a set of three.

". . . In the evening, a band played music out on the end of dock. The little children had fun swimming in the clear lake and riding on the merry-go-round and ferris wheel.

"The means of providing electricity was unique. The engines of the Dan Patch provided transportation to and from the park, and the No. 1 engine of the road, the Augerita, supplied all the electricity for Antler's Park."

The bright era of Dan Patch began to wane during World War I and in 1918, the bankrupt line was purchased by the Minneapolis, Northfield & Southern. That's where I came in.

I can remember those rides on the orange Dan Patch as if they took place yesterday.

The old station was at Seventh street and First avenue N., Minneapolis. (It stands yet, but as a bus depot.) The car ran about 4 p.m. each day. Behind the V-shaped cab was a baggage compartment and behind that the passenger section, with an old-fashioned observation platform at the rear.

The seats were leather, big and deep cushioned, with roll tops that added to the passenger comfort. And there was a peculiar odor in the car, of disinfectant, perhaps; the nearest thing to it is the smell of a cedar closet.

The train began with a leap and snort, and kept jumping all the way to Northfield. With its streamlined snout and noisy engine, it presented an awesome sight rocking and thundering down the track that snaked and wound through what is now Edina and Hopkins past the Auto club into the Minnesota river bottomland and across an interesting trestle that also carried auto traffic.

I can recall that I was always afraid the thing would blow up some day and gave the engine cab a wide berth when I got off.

I can't remember what speeds were attained, but the Dan Patch usually arrived in Northfield about 5:30 p.m. Since I never rode any farther, the rest of the run is mere hearsay.

Students at Carleton and St. Olaf colleges in the 20s will remember the rides they took to special events in the city on chartered Dan Patch cars. On those occasions, a small, black, half-length Dan Patch was used—a spare car. And sometimes it dragged one or two passenger cars behind it—all with open end platforms.

But the highway running alongside the track began to fill up with buses and cars and one by one the old riders were missing from the station stops, many nothing more than little shelters.

Two trains each way daily dwindled to one a day.

Then, on April 30, 1942, Dan Patch made its last run to North-field. Eight passengers rode the orange train that hooted and honked a funereal dirge through the valley, ticking off the familiar, quaint stations.

Freight trains still ply the track today, but the Dan Patch runs only through the musty old records and in the minds of those who rode on it.

A Nightingale on the Prairie

The announcement by the Chicago & North Western railway that its passenger trains No. 201 and 202 from St. Paul to Omaha will be discontinued deserves at least a brief eulogy to the end of an era of railroading.

There will be, when the final notes of the diesel have died away, a void in the darkness, stretching across 400 miles of southwestern Minnesota prairie.

And to me the passing of these trains will come as something of a personal loss.

They were called the Nightingales, and their plaintive song in the still of the night came to be part of life in the villages, towns and cities that grew up along the trackside.

Shakopee, Jordan, Mankato, Lake Crystal, Mountain Lake, Bingham Lake, Windom, Worthington—these are just some of the names on the timetable of the Nightingale.

In voice and speed, no train ever was more aptly named. There was something romantic about the tones pouring out into the silence of the countryside from that shiny, black, high-wheeled locomotive. And when, in its best years, the train was hauled by a steamer, that engine was known for its flight.

It was, as a small boy in one of the towns just mentioned, that I first knew the Nightingale.

I came to regard it as a friend that came and went during the small hours of the night. The train didn't stop in town, but hurtled on through.

And as you lay there in bed on a hot summer night when not a breath stirred and the prairie was wrapped in sleep, the first bars of the Nightingale's call drifted across the bed from the distance like a muted song.

Then, as it came nearer, the whistle grew into a lonesome cry. And the pounding of the drive wheels began shaking the roadbed and it came to your ears as a rushing gale.

Then it was upon the town, its whistle echoing back and forth between the grain elevators and the buildings shook and throbbed to the rhythm of the wheels.

In an instant it was gone again, calling into the night. And gradually the sound subsided until all you could hear was the laboring of the locomotive exhaust climbing a grade southwest of the town.

But, as the Nightingale flew by, it embodied all the glamor and thrills a small boy's mind could conjure up and nothing I have heard since ever came near equalling that.

In later years I rode the Nightingale, when it was a string of varnished Pullmans, a proud thing to watch. In those days the train was a mobile link between St. Paul and the Pacific coast.

The club car was filled with cosmopolites and the coaches with young and old, going west to seek their fortunes. And by the dim light of the old, globe lights on the ceiling, they'd talk about the future and josh the news butcher who sold ham sandwiches and apples.

Long after it no longer flies its course, there will be those along the tracks who will wake with a start on a dark and quiet night and hear again, from some far away place, the Nightingale's melody.

A Railroad Beanerie

In the rapidly ebbing era of the old-time railroad beanerie-hotel, there remains between Chicago and San Francisco only one worth a reputation. And that is the Burlington Hotel, set on a shelf at the foot of Earl Street, just to the left of the Warner Road overpass.

Here I can recommend the coffee at a nickel a cup (refills on the house), the griddle cakes, and a wealth of railroad stories which will stir the blood of any amateur knight of the road.

And a snowladen day, with a north wind biting at the heels, is just the time to repair to the Burlington, one of the coziest spots on the right-of-way.

Whatever it lacks in 20th century decor and custom, the Burlington makes up for in originality.

It is open 24 hours a day, seven days a week, never failing to minister to the wants of a hungry railroader who has just come up from the yards below after a frosty night switching cars.

It has breached the space of time between the old and new in communication, for instance. You see at once a new French-style telephone and also an old-type wall phone, one of the few remaining in use hereabouts.

That is for special calls—incoming only, from the "call boy" in the yards who summons his minions at all hours to come down and start the wheels of a fast or slow freight rolling south or west.

Upstairs in the 12 box-shaped rooms holding 21 beds you will find odd-looking ropes, looped near the windows. These are fire escape ropes, swinging exits to the ground below.

In the regimen of the Burlington, the hours of dawn and 7 p.m. are the noisiest and busiest. These seem to be the intervals when the railroaders swarm into the place.

They climb the long stairs from the sea of red and green switch-lamps below, while others, wiping shaving soap off hastily-trimmed faces, shuffle bleary-eyed into the glare and grope for steaming coffee cups.

"Ham and cakes!"

That is railroad fare at the Burlington at 7 a.m., something to stick to a man's ribs while he rides the cab of a diesel or swings from the icy, iron rungs of a boxcar at the end of a string of freight cars.

Historically, the Burlington has enjoyed a tenure of more than 50 years on the East Side ledge. The original burned to the ground along about 1920.

The new Burlington resembles an Army barracks and quite naturally, since the building is a remnant of old Camp Grant and was brought up to St. Paul in sections.

It nearly reached a disastrous end before it began, however, because the clam shovel which deposited the various parts on their present site released the load prematurely, jumbling things up to a fare-you-well.

It is a wonder that the Burlington's design, then, is a logical as it is.

The Burlington enjoys one more distinction that few other hotels in America can claim.

If you stand on the lawn in front, it is possible to see every form of transportation known to man—the planes at Holman field, trains, boats in the river, cars, buses, trucks, people walking, bicycles and motorcycles.

And every room comes with a view.

[*The Burlington Hotel is now only an empty lot.*]

Tin Goose Comes Home

It was just last Friday afternoon that the two of us stood on the wind-swept apron in front of the hangar and watched the Tin Goose in her homecoming performance at Holman field after 22 years.

Out at the end of the strip, her three motors revved to a shrieking crescendo like the pounding of a thousand tympani. Then the brakes released and the Tin Goose trundled down the runway—barely a few hundred yards, the way it looked—and lifted abruptly into the air.

Her wings flickered a second in a crosswind, then steadied as she climbed free of the current.

The man standing next to me crinkled his leathery face into a smile.

"She's a honey," he said in reverent voice.

It was one of those offbeat moments of history you stumble into by chance. Because the plane was an old Ford Tri-Motor and seeing it landing and taking off on Holman field was like turning back the chapters of aviation history. And the man at my elbow was one of the men who had brought her to fame. Capt. L.S. (Deke) DeLong, 63, senior pilot for Northwest Orient Airlines. And between the plane and the man was a link of friendship that few can understand, save those who fly.

Deke had just climbed out of the plane's cabin before I met him. His old friend, Captain Joe Kimm of Seattle, was flying the Tin Goose at the moment.

They were "checking out" the Tri-Motor in advance of a coast-to-coast flight observing NWA's 30th anniversary.

Deke is the pilot, Joe is co-pilot.

"That's a hot one," said Deke. "Joe is No. 9 on the seniority list and he's going to be my co-pilot. And him flying these new Super G Constellations regular for Northwest."

Deke's face crinkled up again into a smile.

It had been 22 years since Deke had put his hands on the controls of one of those Tri-Motors. In the interim had been the steadily modernized, swift, giant new transports, the DC-4s, Strato-cruisers, DC6-Bs, the "Connies."

"How did it feel when you sat down to fly her again?" I said.

"I'll tell you, boy, it was just like coming home, like I'd never been away," said Deke.

"Maybe they make a lot of noise. But that old ship was the best. Revolutionized the concept of commercial aviation, it did. Most maneuverable darn plane I ever flew. Only thing these new ships have is more speed. That's all."

Deke, like some others, remembered that it was his old friend Charles (Speed) Holman who was the only man ever to loop a Tri-Motor. Did it three times.

And there's another reason why the Tri-Motor is more like a St. Paul plane than a Ford Motor Co. product.

The man who designed it was the late Bill Stout of St. Paul, one of the all-time great inventors and architects of flying machines.

Deke and I watched the Tin Goose out of sight over Holman field and walked over to get a cup of coffee. Deke talked about the span of aviation which he personifies and of which the Tri-Motor is just a bright episode.

Though he has 25,000 hours in the air, 38 years of flying behind him (starting with Jennys in World War I), those hands are as steady when they light a cigarette as those of the youngest and sharpest pilot on the line.

They are firm, deft hands. In 38 years, Deke has held the lives of thousands of passengers in their palms. And never injured a person.

Deke says he still makes his regular run, in a DC-4, to Winnipeg and return. For him every takeoff and every landing is a thrill.

"You know," he said, "I'm just playing at this flying business now. I've lived through the most wonderful part of world history. I came in before the telephone was established and I expect to fly jets before I quit."

"Why," he says, "I can remember when the co-pilot's only job on the Tri-Motor was to hold the controls in a cross wind and pass out the sandwiches, and also the cups to sick passengers. You talk about progress."

Deke and I sat there on a bench in the overhaul hangar corridor. Old friends of his, mechanics and foremen, came up, slapped him on the back and said: "Well, Deke, you all set for next week. Goin' to take her across country? Seem like old times, hey?"

"Wasn't going to take on this flight," said Deke. "They asked what it would take to get me to go and I said: 'Send a pretty stewardess along and I'll consider it. So they give me a Hawaiian girl— you oughta see her hula—an American, a Japanese girl—girl from every country we serve. They're all going along, in native costume. Sure, I'm going."

(Actually Deke gave up his vacation, which he planned to spend at his home down on nearby Grey Cloud island, to make this sentimental journey.)

We were back on the apron again. And from the right came the mighty drone, as Joe Kimm settled the Tri-Motor back on the field.

The Tin Goose waddled proudly and shiny past the line of sleek Air National Guard fighter planes, the trim, modern twin-engine ships parked along the fringe, past a jet—the old saluting the new, with a dip of her wing.

"Isn't she a grand old bird?" said Deke.

Midway at Midnight

Night had fallen hours earlier over the St. Paul Midway district. It came with a misting rain that froze on the ground and mirrored the streets with ice. And sent a chill through layers of clothing.

Most of the buildings, where labor the eight to four people, had long since been emptied, now stood darkly, shrouded by a veil of mist. Abroad in the city, sleep came slowly.

Then, if you looked, there were blobs of light, glowing like balls at scattered places in the Midway, hidden, some of them, back behind the façades along busy University Avenue.

These are the lights from the world's third largest trucking center, whose hub is the sprawling Midway of St. Paul. Through the night it—almost alone in the area—is alive, manned by a force of men and women whose work day is turned topsy-turvy, but who catch the romance of working at night.

Hour after hour, from the loading platforms of a hundred truck lines, the trucks and trailers—hundreds of them—fan out from the hub, disappearing into the night along the spokes—the highways that lead in four directions.

Shoes from Red Wing, bound for Montevideo; special feed earmarked for Dr. A.J. Eckstein of New Ulm; pipe fittings for Plato Plumbing and Heating at Jordan; poultry supplies for the Farmers Market at Winthrop; sweeping compound for Parrott Hardware in Owatonna.

Let's see some of it close up.

You have to step lively to keep out of the way of the little power lift trucks—"Jeeps" they call them—that scoot back and forth across the dock at Witte's Transportation, 2334 University.

They take the freight from one side of the dock and distribute it to the right trailers, each marked with a destination.

"We'll have trucks leaving until 1 a.m. for Rochester, La Crosse, Preston and Grand Meadow," I am told.

Back in the office, men and women keep pace with the work out on the docks as they process freight bills of lading.

As you walk into the garage, where repairs are made and maintenance handled, the damp, night air sends a gust across the platform and you huddle into the collar of your coat.

Out in the locker room a driver is finishing a sandwich before he takes the Preston run.

Four blocks away, the operations room of Glendenning Motorways is humming as the night dispatcher steps over to shake hands.

Glendenning is a pioneer firm and one of the few whose president is a woman.

Along one wall are teletype machines, connecting Glendenning terminals at New Lisbon and Milwaukee, Wisconsin; Duluth, Sioux Falls, Brainerd, Winnipeg, Crookston, Fargo, and Grand Forks.

On the docks, you sidestep freight piles, skitter out of the way of the "jeeps."

"Some nights," the dock foreman says, "we have to put our loads of freezable goods in the garage to keep them warm, then turn on the cooling machinery in the trailers to make sure it doesn't get too hot."

The "garage" is a mammoth series of buildings where Glendenning maintains its fleets, self-sufficient even to body rebuilding, painting and complete rebuilding of motors.

The night garage foreman is proud of his shop as he moves from one department to the other. There's a feeling of power as you walk past the big truck cabs, examining their mighty engines. Over here a mechanic is busy repairing a radiator leak on a truck that will leave after midnight for the north.

The cluster of men at the parts window is welcoming the coffee man, whose steaming urn is quickly emptied.

The clock is nearing a new day at Murphy Motor Freight where the sign on the arch reads: "Through these portals pass the safest drivers in the world." And on the bumpers of the trucks are such slogans as: "Beer Today, Gone Tomorrow ;" "Don't Be Half Safe."

At Murphy no "jeeps," but a monorail system of little freight trucks that move endlessly in an oblong circle, running at least two blocks in length along the dock, one of the longest in the country. As they reach their assigned stall, they are lifted off the track, pushed into the trailer for unloading.

It's more like noon than midnight at Murphy where men and women work at high speed on the multitudinous paper work, office lights blazing out into the icy night.

"Many of these women are housewives by day and work here at night—some until 3 a.m.," says the operations chief. "Here, meet one of them."

"Been driving 13 years," says a driver of Tracy. "It's like a fever that gets in your blood—truck driving. Especially at night. There's something fascinating about this business at night."

And there is.

Yellowstone Park at the Corner of Selby and Virginia

As they hurried past it last week, only a few persons may have paused to notice the big "SOLD" sign posted on the faded wood sides of that imposing building at Selby and Virginia.

In the last years, it has become something of a relic of another episode in the history of the city, just as are so many other structures spotted in this section of the Hill district.

"I wonder," some may have meditated, "whether there is a story about that place?"

In reply, one could have asked them whether they might have—in a drawer at home—a postcard purchased in Yellowstone Park. Or whether they might have seen, at one time or another, a classic picture of "Old Faithful" geyser doing its stuff.

For here, in this building of curiosity, was processed a great bulk of the postcards sold at the concession stands in Yellowstone Park since 1895.

Here, at the turn of the century, was the largest and most completely-equipped photographic studio in the Northwest.

It was called the Haynes Photo Studio and the design and architecture were the fruits of a dream, realized by one of the West's most fabulous and colorful personalities—F. Jay Haynes, who pioneered with a camera as others pioneered for riches and land.

And the studio at Selby and Virginia is only one of the marks he left along the trail that criss-crossed the great Northwest from St. Paul to Puget Sound.

Long before F. Jay Haynes created this work of art on a St. Paul street corner, he had pocketed fame.

He was the official photographer for President Chester A. Arthur's expedition through Yellowstone Park in 1883. And by then he had discovered and originated the Yellowstone Park picture concession which his son, Jack, still holds.

A mountain, Mt. Haynes, in Madison canyon, was named for him.

His *Yellowstone Guidebook* is still the "Bible" of the park. The rare photographs of park views and its animals in the latest editions are all Haynes-inspired.

There is a story told about the classic photograph of "Old Faithful." Allegedly, Haynes and his compatriots threw tin cans and sticks and stones into the crater in an effort to irritate the great geyser into reaching for untold heights. Which it did.

F. Jay established a close liaison with the builders of the Northern Pacific railway and he was the official photographer when, on Sept. 8, 1883, the golden spike was driven connecting the two ends of that transcontinental railway near Garrison, Montana.

The first and only Palace studio railway car in the world was owned by him. He outfitted it as a mobile photo studio and brought the marvels of photography to residents along the line.

Perhaps his association with the NP brought him to St. Paul. He'd been something of a Minnesotan from earlier days in Moorhead. And in 1889, F. Jay packed up his studio in Fargo and moved to St. Paul, where he established himself at Sixth and Jackson.

But he'd always hankered for his own-styled studio. And what you see, at Selby and Virginia, fading like some of the old portraits that hung on the walls, was his idea.

It was opened in 1895 and there are, still alive in the city, many residents of long years who recall the grandeur of sitting, stiff-necked and fidgeting, in front of a Haynes studio camera, looking for the "birdie."

But the heart of the studio was its Yellowstone Park business and who can tell how many millions of postcards were printed and packaged there?

Last week, when they began cleaning out the old files, there were boxes and boxes of old negatives, plates and photographs, brought up from the musty basement.

The inside of the studio was luxurious, even unto the last. I remember stopping in about two years ago one afternoon to talk to E.W. Hunter, a man now in his 80s, who stayed with the building to the last.

Mr. Hunter, by the way, was one of the country's finest photographers. His dramatic photos of Yellowstone Park bears and scenery added to the prestige of Haynes' work.

That afternoon he was alone in the studio, dim and cold. But the two of us shared again some of the studio's finest moments and I shall never forget the glazed, tile fireplaces that gave it an air of antiquated opulence.

But it must have been a busy place of fashionable cars and carriages at the pillared doorway during those first years of this century.

Its creator, F. Jay, stayed to watch until 1921 when he died quietly on March 10 in his home at 601 Dayton, within walking distance of the studio.

His son, Jack, took his father's place behind the lenses. Gradually, the business was moved west to the Haynes Log Cabin studio in the park, with headquarters now at Bozeman, Montana, where Jack lives. Yet, sentimentally perhaps, the St. Paul studio was kept operating until this past Oct. 1.

In recent years youngsters in the Selby-Western neighborhood used to call it a haunted house.

And give it a wide berth when they passed on dark and moonless nights.

And in a sense they were right. For that old building is surely haunted by memories of men who have done more than any others to tell the story of Yellowstone Park to the world.

From the corner of Selby and Virginia.

Bricks and Mortar

Fitzgerald Brownstone Still Houses Vivid Memories

Some pictures frame in my mind when I pass the old "F. Scott Fitzgerald" brownstone at 599 Summit Avenue with the "For Sale" sign. I walk up close to read the plaque that says the old charmer is on the National Register of Historic Places, ever since 1972.

I remember that damp, chilly afternoon when the representative came from the Department of Interior's Chicago office to present the plaque to Ethel Cline, the owner who now wants to pass on the home to another generation.

I'd known Cline ever since a day in the late 1940s, when an English professor from a Southern university on his honeymoon called the *Pioneer Press* city desk. I was assistant city editor then and he wanted to know where F. Scott Fitzgerald had lived the longest in St. Paul.

Cline agreed to give him a tour when I called, and that began a friendship cemented by the ghost of a man we both admired.

In fact, Cline became so immersed in F. Scott Fitzgerald lore that she reveled in conducting informal tours, and, though her privacy was often broken by the doorbell at all hours, she was always the gracious hostess.

She called me one day in 1972 to say that through the good offices of Russell Fridley, director of the state Historical Society, the brownstone had been designated a National Historic site. She was ecstatic.

Would I like to come for the ceremony? There would be low tea served later in the English tradition.

Of course I accepted. We sat around a coffee table in the parlor and the young man from the Department of the Interior presented Ethel with the certificate, and then the plaque was affixed and we posed for pictures.

She had hoped that the Fitzgerald's daughter, Scottie, would come, as she later did.

We looked at the scrapbooks and then Ethel took us on a tour.

She led us to the third floor, front bedroom and with a dramatic flourish said, "And this is where Scott wrote and finished 'This Side of Paradise'."

We all sat at the desk, peering out the window on Summit Avenue trying to visualize how it was when Scott sat there.

At the time he was wooing Zelda by mail. It was 1919. And when they married, he brought her back to St. Paul at intervals, but never to 599 Summit Avenue.

There have been only a few other times when I have felt as close to the Fitzgeralds as I did that day.

One summer in the mid-1960s, I was commanding a media team through Army maneuvers in the Carolinas as a reserve officer and wound up in Spartanburg, where I spent a nostalgic afternoon with Fred Wolfe, brother of author Thomas Wolfe. Fred knew Scott and Zelda and told me how it was in Asheville, North Carolina, the night Zelda burned to death in a fire in a mental institution there.

"She had been staying at the Wolfe home, and if she'd only behaved and stayed with us, she never would have died and the whole ending to the Fitzgerald story might have been different," Fred kept saying that day.

I had the feeling of closeness the day I found "F. Scott Fitzgerald" autographed and burned into the wood on the big bar in the basement rathskeller of the University Club.

And the time I was gathering the history of the White Bear Yacht Club and some of the people who were contemporaries of Fitzgerald when he cavorted and lived there described where he sat, where he wrote, where he walked and how it was at those fabled, raucous parties.

Then there was the evening in Paris when my wife and I found the present Shakespeare & Co. bookstore made famous by Sylvia Beach in the 1920s and 30s as a rendezvous for all the expatriate American writers, artists and musicians.

The owner, who had reopened the store after World War II, kept us a long time talking about Fitzgerald when he found out I was from St. Paul.

"People come in so often," he said, "and want to talk about Scott and those years with Hemingway, James Joyce and Gertrude Stein. I often feel that they are all back there lurking in the shadows."

I suspect that whoever acquired 599 Summit Avenue will have the same feeling from time to time.

Crews Tear Down Plaza, Not Memories

In the half century plus of roaming the streets of Downtown St. Paul, I've watched the city reshaped at least once, and now and then the second time around.

Like Hamm Plaza at Sixth and St. Peter.

I walked out of the Skyway in front of the Hamm building on a recent afternoon and watched demolition crews ripping down Hamm Plaza park with its massive waterfall sculpture, which I once dubbed the world's biggest public shower.

Just the same, it was a blow for cleanliness and relief from the heat among the street people, who often stood under it on hot summer nights.

As I joined the sidewalk superintendents watching the demise of the square, I wondered if any of them remembered how it was before Hamm Plaza, when that triangle of land was the old central bus depot?

When I arrived in the city in August of 1939, the Greyhound lane was along one side of the triangle. The Jefferson bus lines used the second lane, and the Twin City Rapid Transit buses had the third.

There wasn't a lot of parking space along the curbside, so at busy times buses quite often parked two and three abreast.

Inside were the ticket windows, the waiting room and, I believe, a modest lunch counter and newsstand.

That triangle was like a hub, a core of Downtown life. Especially around 5 p.m., when the Greyhound and Jefferson buses headed out state would load. As I recall, the major Greyhound terminal was in Minneapolis. A shuttle ran between St. Paul and Minneapolis, making connections for west and southwest. Buses east and north started in Minneapolis and stopped in St. Paul on their way out of the area.

Jefferson line buses always headed south to Northfield, Faribault, Albert Lea, Austin and Mason City, Iowa, from St. Paul.

You should have seen the crowds. Fares were cheaper than trains, passenger airplane service was still in its embryonic stage and the automobile had not yet begun to clog the roads.

Besides, buses would stop at crossroads trains never got near.

So the St. Paul bus depot was overcrowded from the day it opened; travellers and the city fathers complained that we needed a new and bigger facility.

But meantime, I have some fond memories of that old depot.

Like the night of the infamous Armistice Day Blizzard of November 11, 1940.

I was going to the University of Minnesota then and working nights at the *Pioneer Press*. That day was a holiday from classes, so I took the streetcar from the campus to Downtown St. Paul about noon, when the rain was changing to snow.

By nightfall the storm was raging full fury and Bill Greer, the city editor, was making arrangements to house the staff in the Lowry Hotel.

Not for me.

I wasn't about to spend the night in a hotel when I could be snug and warm in my bed on campus in Pioneer Hall. Besides, I had classes the next morning.

So, foolishly, I went out into the storm and got as far as Seventh and Wabasha, where crowds were waiting for streetcars that never came.

I heard somebody say: "Buses are still running to Minneapolis on University Avenue."

So I slogged a block over to the bus depot. Sure enough, there stood a St. Paul-Minneapolis bus, full of people peering out of steaming windows.

I managed to get on and the driver said: "Well, folks, we're going to try it. If we can get up the St. Peter Street hill, we may have a chance." (St. Peter was a two-way street then.)

He put the bus in low gear and off we spun, skimming through the drifts quite easily until we started up the hill at College Avenue. The bus wheels spun to a stop. It looked hopeless until someone shouted: "Let's get out and push."

And, by golly, we pushed that bus up the St. Peter Street hill, while the driver gunned the motor. At the top of the hill, he stopped, we all got back on and off we went up Rice to University, zigzagging around stalled cars and marooned streetcars. At Western and Dale, Lexington and Snelling, those who wanted to get off jumped on the run as the driver slowed the bus. Most were going to downtown Minneapolis.

When he crossed Oak and Washington on the campus, I told him I wanted to get off. He slowed the bus, opened the door, and I jumped into a snowbank as the bus continued through the storm.

Ten minutes later I called the *Pioneer Press* city desk from my dormitory room.

"I made it," I said.

I was the only one on the staff that night who got home.

The other day as I stood watching the demolition of Hamm Plaza, I had to think about that wild ride in a night of storm-borne tempest.

[*The Hamm Plaza was then being cleared for a newly designed sculptural arrangement.*]

High Bridge Played Prominent Role in City Story

The keening about the passing of the High Bridge has begun to fade into a wealth of legends about the old span, which are starting to be told these nights in the pubs and bars along Fort Road and out Randolph Avenue.

A lot of the barroom historians remember when the bridge actually did fall once, and tell about the hot August night in 1904 during a terrible storm, then called a cyclone, but probably a tornado or windstorm. That one not only rent the bridge asunder near the south end, but also wrecked devastation through downtown St. Paul, demolishing the old Tivoli beer garden and hall at Third and Wabasha streets.

A lot of second- and third-generation versions of "eyewitness" stories have been bandied about at Mancini's and DeGidio's bars and also Skarda's these last few weeks.

And a few even hauled out yellowed photos and clippings about how the bridge looked, and everybody commented on the strange fact that nobody was either under or on the bridge at the time it fell.

They spliced it back together again. In the 1950s, when it was undergoing one of its infrequent refurbishings, I walked out on the middle one night and saw the splice marks, the rivet plates, the welded seams, whatever.

Pretty scary.

But not as scary as the spring morning I crawled around in the framework, helping the Public Works bridge crew hang navigation lights. There may be a few of the workers around who remember that. It was as close to tightrope and high-wire walking as I ever got, and those fellows were like monkeys.

My shoes seemed to be greased.

The bridge foreman, Bob Rasmussen, liked to reminisce about the Great Depression in the 1930s, when "so many people jumped off the High Bridge you had to take a number and get in line."

In fact, that was how the phrase "I feel like taking the High Bridge" originated.

The story about how it got its name may be apocryphal. It is said that the bridge initially was called simply the Smith Avenue Bridge because it connected both ends of Smith Avenue, honoring a mayor by that name.

But there was another Smith, J. George Smith, who owned a candy store on Sixth Street. He also had one of the first automobiles in town.

To test its power, he drove it from the lower to the upper end of the bridge in high gear one day, and thus it got the name High Bridge.

Along about midnight at McGovern's bar, you get a half-dozen other versions of that story.

There is also the unsubstantiated story that Charles (Speed) Holman, fabled flier, a founder and first chief pilot of Northwest Airlines, flew under the High Bridge upside down.

I asked his widow, Dee Holman, about it once, and she said she wouldn't put it past him, but couldn't say if the feat ever happened.

She did say he had flown her right side up under the Mendota Bridge on their honeymoon.

One of my favorite stories, related to me by the man involved, is about one who went off the High Bridge and survived to become a prominent businessman and philanthropist.

His name was Richard Lilly, and he was president of the First National Bank of St. Paul.

One evening in the 1930s, Lilly was driving home, down the High Bridge, when his car skidded and went through a guard rail at the lower end. It plunged toward what is now Shepard Road, but landed instead in a huge Northern States Power Co. coal pile.

They rushed Lilly to old Ancker Hospital.

That incident changed his life.

One Christmas week in about 1960, I happened to be out at the old Christ Child School for Exceptional Children on Summit Avenue, across from the College of St. Thomas.

Lilly had been a benefactor, and he was at the Christmas party.

"You know," he said, "when I was lying in Ancker Hospital after my accident, I decided that God had given me a second chance, and I wanted to express my gratitude in some way. And my assistance here is one of those ways."

There were others, but Lilly wasn't the kind to wear these things on his sleeve.

All of which suggests the High Bridge played a lot bigger role in the drama and story of the city than merely being a span from one side of the Mississippi River to the other.

And while the "West Side Connection" may no longer be in use, there is a traffic jam of ghosts on it almost every night.

[*There is now a new, third High Bridge, which opened in 1986.*]

Pioneer Lawyer Parlayed His French into Choice Bit of St. Paul Property

Sometimes it pays to know another language.

At 4:30 p.m. last June 19, a piece of property at Seventh and Robert streets changed hands—for the first time in 128 years. The legacy of pioneer settler William Pitt Murray became a financial pie cut into 14 slices.

The story is woven into the history of Robert Street, the man for whom it is named and the romance of the city's past.

Murray's great-grandson, James Harrison, told it to me.

We went back to a summer's day in 1856, and a tiny frame building at what is now 10th and Robert where Murray, a young attorney, had hung out his shingle. Murray was visited that day by Louis Robert, French-Canadian entrepreneur, fur trader and steamboat line operator.

Robert had a strange request and an equally unusual offer.

If Murray would translate an important document from English into French, Robert would pay him with a piece of property, "provided you build a good house on it. Some day that land will be worth a lot of money," he prophesied.

Looking over the lot, with a brook running through a marshy low area, young Murray might have been a bit dubious.

But he agreed to the terms.

He put his house on the site and brought his new bride to live in it and it was their home for 35 years.

It was also the future home of The Golden Rule department store, later Donaldson's-Golden Rule.

For Murray and his descendants, Louis Robert had been a prophet.

As Harrison, who handled the transfer to the Hemar student loan service firm, says, "That property certainly was much more valuable, in the thousands of dollars, than even Louis Robert could have dreamed."

He shied from specific figures, but said, "in 1911, when Murray's will was probated, the property was placed at $250,000." That value has yo-yoed with economic conditions.

The sale also ended the saga of perhaps the longest family-held property in downtown St. Paul.

Murray wanted it that way. He wanted his family to have the property as his legacy to them forever. And his descendants kept that faith until recently.

"They were always able to lease that northwest corner of Seventh and Robert, first to The Golden Rule, then Donaldson's," says Harrison.

"But the time finally came when we knew that eventually the property would be acquired by eminent domain. The building had been vacant, and the city wanted it made available for the Hemar Company."

Harrison, who is executive director of the Minnesota-Wisconsin Boundary Area Commission, says he thought it was the time to agree to a sale if possible. And because of his background, the family elected him to do the honors.

He had to get the approval from 14 of them, scattered across the country.

"There were a few who were reluctant, sort of sentimental about it. We all were. But eventually, they all agreed."

There were some bonuses.

In doing his research, Harrison's mother came up with an old family trunk. Inside, Harrison found a letter from William Pitt Murray, describing the incident.

"On the 23rd day of December 1849, I arrived in St. Paul with an English sovereign and 40 cents in my pocket. During the winter I was fortunate enough to get business to pay my board and pay for my washing. No one knew how poor I was except myself.

"The next year a little more business came to me. In one of my cases, I received a land warrant for my fee. With this I entered 160 acres of land. I was doing a very good business—and as I thought with economy might support a wife—I married your mother and brought her to St. Paul. The first year we lived in a rented home on the corner of Fourth and Jackson Street. Before the year was out I bought a small new house on the corner of Robert and 10th Street. We lived in this house until the summer of 1856 when I had a chance to sell it for $3,500.

"Louis Robert then offered to make me a present of Lot 12, being one (of) the lots where The Golden Rule stands, if I would build a good house on it. (The French translation of the document was described in another item of family history.) I sold my Robert Street property and built upon 7th Street, where we lived for 35 years."

Murray became as successful as that property. He was an outstanding attorney, a political figure and the first St. Paul City Attorney.

And it was he who secured the 99-year lease on that corner that was in force until the sale.

William Pitt Murray is buried in Oakland cemetery.

That plot, as Harrison says, is all the land that belongs to him now.

History Hotel

Some persons, riding into the Loop just after sunrise, view it as a massive castle on the Rhine, rising out of the morning mist.

The well traveled may see in it at once the opulent luxury of the Metropole in Brussels, the Grand National in Lucerne. With the bay windows, iron grillwork around the little balconies, chimneys dotting the roof, once spiraling wisps of smoke from the ornate place in the high-ceilinged rooms.

The fireplaces are now merely decorative, the chimneys long cool. Yet Phil Lawrence, present manager of the Ryan hotel at Sixth and Robert—it is the Ryan about which I am speaking—

recalls when it was a chore of the bellmen to carry buckets of coal and wood to the rooms with fireplaces.

Stand in the famous old Ryan bar, at the rear of the building, and look at your image in the massive, mahogany-trimmed mirror, and somebody will mention the legend of John L. Sullivan who cracked it with his mighty fist on a dare. The legend is fact and I last heard the story from one who was there, the late Earl Jones, a waiter who became a fixture in the Ryan himself before a hit-run driver cut off his life in the 80s a few years ago.

Which story also was recalled a year or so ago when a boxing ring was set up in the marble-pillared lobby and Del Flanagan worked out each noon before at least two of his matches. About where Mary Garden sang impromptu opera.

Those pillars, by the way, are not real marble, but synthetic covering, installed by Italian artists who imitated the real McCoy down to realistic cracks in the surface.

If your imagination needs exciting, walk up the wide staircase, covered by deep carpeting, lined by heavy, oak banisters, and you achieve the same feeling of grandeur—on the same steps—that President Grover Cleveland must have felt in 1887, or some of those in attendance at the banquet in 1888 marking Bishop John Ireland's elevation to archbishop, or, perhaps the night they honored James J. Hill in 1893 upon the completion of the Great Northern railway to the Pacific coast.

I got the feeling of the Ryan's magnificent role in St. Paul hostelry history the other day. I sat at a business luncheon in one of the private dining rooms over some of catering manager Harry Keeney's lentil soup and prime ribs, served on heavy dinner service, and looked out of the window through the crimson drapes. I was almost surprised to see motorcars instead of horse-drawn carriages and drays clattering on the street below.

As I looked around the room, at the marble-framed fireplace, I remembered from my own experience an evening I once spent there as the guest of some swashbuckling Montana livestockmen who'd ridden in on the annual fall parade of sheep trains and were celebrating the harvest.

And other evenings, election nights, when the same dining rooms were turned into party victory quarters and the faithful came by to pay homage to their champions of the ballot boxes. Receptions long before my time when the actresses and actors, famed singers and European royalty held "court" on the mezzanine.

What I am trying to say is that between some point in the Alleghenies and San Francisco, I doubt that there ever was or still is a hotel like the Ryan, which has kept neck and neck with progress without losing the almost vanished charm of the great hotels that flourished between 1885 when it was built and the early 1900s.

Though telephone operators and cashier may work under 1959-style drop ceilings in the lobby, and the new elevator is the last word in modernism, the seasoned atmosphere of the Ryan has not been lost, just kept up by its present owners, Yale and Harry Johnson, who recognize that age can be a useful trademark, not a handicap.

The existence of the Ryan is due to a gentleman, Dennis Ryan, a mining magnate, who built the six stories—plus lobby—in 1885. There is debate about who signed No. 1 on the register for the first of the 300 rooms. Some sources say it was Ryan himself. But another lists General James Heaton Baker of Mankato.

Dennis Ryan set a tradition of good eating which has followed the Ryan all the days of its life. He opened with a banquet too long to detail, but there were such viands as Kennebec salmon, larded sweetbreads, teal duck, champagne jelly, tenderloin of beef, spring lamb, green turtle soup, washed down with vins de Pasto, de Graves, cardinal punch and finally French coffee.

All this was served in what is now the Marquette ballroom, which has later been the setting for some of the most fabulous affairs of city and state.

Adding a fillip to the first banquet was the fact that it was served on some $10,000 worth of specially-kilned Limoges china, pieces of which were stored in the hotel vault until a few years ago, but used only five times. They since have been disposed of.

The Ryan's reputation for setting a good table has never been in doubt since. There are, presently flourishing, five eateries, more than in any hotel in this part of the country. And one has a choice between linen and gleaming silverware with menu to match or the sandwich bar toward the rear where the corned beef sandwich is a talking piece. Its Sunday smorgasbord matches the rare items Dennis Ryan's chefs prepared in 1885.

A chill may run up your spine when you learn that, just before World War II, there was serious talk of tearing asunder those three-foot thick walls in favor of a parking lot.

For those old walls, which would spin many a story if they could talk, daily perform yeoman service in providing lodging for the night.

[*The Ryan Hotel was demolished in 1962, and the Minnesota Mutual Life building took its place.*]

Punch at the Ryan

The Ryan Hotel, whose Roman pillars in the lobby have looked at many a piece of history being made since the 1880s, a few years back witnessed the punch being put back into boxing in St. Paul.

What was billed as the best free noon-hour show in town was staged in the Ryan by the principals in a big boxing event.

The lads worked out in a huge ring, erected in the center of the Ryan lobby. And they played to a standing room crowd only during the week—mainly because if you sat down in the easy chairs you couldn't see.

I went around to see the spectacle and it was a good thing I got there before the fight began. The sports in town had just about filled the lobby and spectators were draped up the wide staircase leading to the mezzanine.

A fellow standing next to me said he estimated the crowd at about 500—including cigars.

"Madam Schumann-Heink didn't draw like this back when she was at the Ryan," said the fellow. "And neither did Mary Garden."

"Of course they weren't sparring in a ring wearing tights either," I said.

Kid Gavilan, the Cuban fighter, came through the crowd then. He was a dazzling success in a red, white and blue robe. The Kid nodded and bowed and climbed into the ring.

"He oughta have the title," said a man behind me.

Jim Hegerle, the Kid's sparring partner, marched in about then.

These noontime sparring matches were a little confusing.

Wednesday's principals changed partners for the Ryan exhibitions, so that Mr. Hegerle punched with Mr. Gavilan and Del Flanagan traded fists with Tommy Swan. In the Auditorium they were reversed so that it came out Mr. Gavilan fighting Mr. Flanagan in the main event and Mr. Hegerle and Mr. Swan in the preliminary.

But I guess everybody knows that.

Well, Harry (Doc) Adams, veteran St. Paul fight trainer, got into the ring then, called "time" and Gavilan and Hegerle went to work. They looked to me like they were standing still until I discovered I was watching a pillar instead of the sparring. So I moved around to the other side to get a better look at the play.

Mr. Gavilan put on a good performance. So did Mr. Hegerle. Their gloves powed together, Mr. Gavilan took time out to lecture the crowd about scenery in Cuba. Mr. Hegerle waved to a few friends in the audience; then they began slamming each other again.

Crowd reaction was varied. One fellow kept bobbing his head with the fighters. Another lit the cork end of a cigaret and everybody acted polite and applauded only at the end of a round.

By this time the Ryan lobby was like an old-time, smoke-filled gym, or, as someone said: "Mayhem Manor." Harry Adams came over and said it reminded him a lot of the Rose Room gym in the Hamm building many years ago.

"These exhibitions are really bringing boxing back to St. Paul," he said. "I mean these here in the Ryan. This is real promotion and it's going over big. Look at the mob. Last Sunday, the boys worked out in the Marquette room upstairs and 400 paid a quarter to watch. Now if that isn't enthusiasm."

I could see the sight was warming Harry's fighting heart. He's been in the boxing business 40 years now. Billy Light, My Sullivan, Charley Retzlaff and Jack Gibbons were some of the boxers in his training history.

Jack Raleigh, the fight promoter, stood on the fringe of the crowd. He looked like his name was "Happy."

It was Jack's idea to build up enthusiasm for boxing matches by holding sparring sessions in the Ryan lobby.

"This ought to be a good one Wednesday night," he said. "The gate is a whopper right now. I think we can do $45,000."

Mr. Gavilan and Mr. Hegerle had ceased their bickering in the ring and Gavilan went into his dance and rope skipping.

"We give him about 45 minutes and then Flanagan comes on with Swan for the same kind of workout," said Jack.

I don't think the Ryan guests from out of town were quite sure whether they were in a hotel or Madison Square Garden with beds.

I remember one fellow who was trying to check out at the cashier's cage. Every time he started to write a check for the tab, the crowd surged against him, jerking the pen in his hand.

Finally he squeezed himself up against the counter, reached for his wallet and took out some cash.

As he eased his way toward the door, I thought I heard him say: "It was a great fight, Ma! I won."

Thirteenth Street Saga

There isn't much left of the old Thirteenth Street neighborhood, below the Capitol, except some grown-over foundations. The houses are all gone and the street is a tree-lined wilderness in the twilight between the past and urban renewal.

But every now and again you come back to Thirteenth street because of a story that began there. This is one of them. I didn't hear it on Thirteenth. Only the birds talk there now. I got it one night when I'd gone over to the St. Louis Park theater in St. Louis Park for a premiere. I didn't watch the movie, but instead sat up in the office and talked to Harold Field, one of the theater's owners.

Harold and his two brothers are building a chain of theaters, 17 by now, 10 indoor, seven outdoor, all in Iowa except the one in St. Louis Park. There is a parallel between the chain the Field brothers are building and the one their father built.

You may have never heard of the Field boys' father—he didn't use that name. But mention the name Finkelstein and Ruben and you stir memories of the most glorious theater net in Northwest show business. Well, Moses Finkelstein was Harold Field's father and they all lived on Thirteenth Street many years ago when it was a top drawer neighborhood of families making a small start up the pyramid.

Moses Finkelstein came to Thirteenth Street about 1887 from Lithuania—a jeweler, who opened a shop on E. Seventh across from The Golden Rule. And in time M. L. Finkelstein Jewelers was one of the finest of its kind in the city. In fact there still are clocks ticking time with the Finkelstein trademark on the cases.

In 1912 Moses owned a piece of property midway between Wabasha and Cedar, where Newman's store now stands. One day a man named I. H. Ruben, who owned a theater in Des Moines, came to St. Paul to visit Moses Finkelstein. He wanted to start a theater on the Seventh Street property.

"But my father was a gambler," said Harold. He joined forces with Ruben and they built the Princess theater—the first one. That was expanded later into the second Princess.

Mama Finkelstein was horrified at the thought of her family being in the show business and forbade her sons to attend opening night. She could have saved her breath. When he passed his 62nd birthday not long ago, Harold completed 43 years in show business.

After the Princess came the Majestic on Cedar, with an entrance on Seventh. Finkelstein and Ruben moved up Seventh beyond Wabasha and opened the Palace, now the Orpheum. It was the late John W. Norton, pioneer real estate man, who assisted them in this venture. And it was he who interested William Hamm, Sr. in associating himself with the theatermen.

Those were heydays for show houses in St. Paul. There were vaudeville shows 11 weeks a year on the stages. Harold Field, meanwhile, cut his eyeteeth on props and curtains, took the University of Minnesota glee club on tour in 1915 or '16, as a student, and helped Mrs. Carlyle Scott establish the University Artists Course series.

Harold rejoined Finkelstein and Ruben after college. At its peak, the chain numbered 180 theaters in Minnesota, Wisconsin and the Dakotas. It was the nation's largest theater chain and, in the history of the American motion picture industry, ranked as a pioneer, never since equalled in size or stature.

The name "Finkelstein and Ruben" became a byword for theatergoers. In fact today it still is as well-known, despite the fact that the circuit was sold in 1928 and Moses Finkelstein died in 1930.

It wasn't until after his father's death that Harold changed his name to Field. "It was the original family name," he says. "My father wanted to change his to Field, too, but he was too well-established as Finkelstein."

Harold and his two brothers began all over again, from scratch, building their own chain, starting in the depression with the Spencer theater in Spencer, Iowa.

Not many persons link them with the famed old name of Finkelstein and Ruben. That is the way they want it. Although most of the chain is in Iowa, the Park is the "home office."

"We built this one to locate our headquarters in the Twin Cities," says Harold. "There's a little sentimentality connected with it."

The Park, by the way, now is managed by a third generation of Finkelsteins-Fields—Harold's son, Martin, who has the same initials as his pioneer motion pictureman grandfather—M. L. F.

And it all began on Thirteenth Street.

Requiem for the Coliseum

They called it the world's largest dance floor.

Three generations of the city ice-skated, roller-skated and danced on it during the oddest, most hectic 38 years of fun, fads and fancies ever recorded.

Its marquee dazzled the eyes of dance-stepping thousands with the biggest name bands ever paraded through St. Paul.

If you had a dollar for every baseball that bounced off its roof—blasted from old Lexington park—you could buy out half the town.

And now they have torn it down and only an empty strip of ground marks the place where the Coliseum once stood on Lexington Parkway near University.

There are many who still rub their eyes and can't believe that the Coliseum isn't there when they pass by. For there have been few buildings which will be remembered so long by so many. Remembered, I say, because the human mind tends to retain the pleasant things in memory and the Coliseum was a place for those.

The night they packed 5,000 persons into the place to hear Ben Bernie and the people sat around at the tables, drinking pop and near beer, some of it spiked with bootleg alcohol.

And I wonder how many persons in the city and scattered across the globe danced to the music of their first "name" band at the Coliseum? Orchestras of Jack Teagarden, Lawrence Welk, Ben Pollack, "Fats" Waller. And there were other names that shone down from the big sign outside—the Andrews Sisters, the Egyptian Serenaders, the White Brothers and Stendel.

There were those nights when Joe Billo played like Clyde McCoy and Clyde McCoy played like Joe Billo. And Katherine Olinger, now a St. Paul policewoman, stood at the door, taking tickets and chaperoning the young womanhood in their chiffon dresses and boyish bobs and wearing the original chemise look of the 1920s.

You could always get a laugh out of the signs on the posts which said: "Park your gum here." Because a lot of patrons did.

It was $3.50 a couple on "big name band" nights and $5.00 on New Year's eve and every Wednesday night was "horse and buggy night" when early arrivals drew for a chance to ride through the city in a surrey with a fringe on top.

And later some of the crowd moved over to the Boulevards of Paris cafe and night club, whose Parisian decor was as close to Paris as most of the visitors got.

The Boulevards was a complement to the Coliseum and its notoriety was heightened during the city's "gangster era" because the big names in gangland liked the best and the Boulevard had it. A supermarket stands there now.

St. Paul danced through the Charleston, the Bunny hop, and the Foxtrot in the Coliseum and a madcap crazy sort of fad called "marathon dancing."

It lasted a month, 24 hours a day, and spectators came and went by day and night to watch the weary couples, alternating heads on each other's shoulders, dozing and dancing. And some of the sporting set sat on the sidelines making "book" on the outcome.

The names that go with the Coliseum are legion. It was the dream of the late John W. Norton, all-time giant of real estate in the city. When he bought the Lexington baseball park in 1918, John also bought the land around it and built the Coliseum as an ice rink to round out his recreation center.

Then a young man named Johnny Lane walked onto the Coliseum stage. He leased the building and, until his death a few years ago, Johnny Lane and the Coliseum were synonymous. It was "Johnny Lane's" Coliseum and never any other way. He died there as he had lived there.

It was in 1921 that the ice rink was scraped off and a dance floor installed.

And thereby hangs a never-before-published tale: When the floor was built, the supports were set a little too far apart on the bare ground.

The result was a wavy or swaying effect on the floor that might have ruined the future of the Coliseum, except that Johnny shrewdly turned this mistake into an advantage. He simply billed the Coliseum as the place with the "Floor that Sways With Motion." It was a private joke among the employees, who called it the "Floor That Sways With Commotion." But the legend was born that the floor was set on a rubber base and it became famous throughout the country.

But there are other names—Earl Smith, now a deputy sheriff, who managed the place for Johnny until 1939, and Sam Specktor, who took up the reins when Johnny died and was there at the end. For Johnny and Sam, the Coliseum played a new role in its golden years— as a roller skating rink. And so the kids whose mothers and fathers danced the "Big Apple" came back to skate to jive and swing.

A bright, new shopping center has gone up where it stood. And while there should be nostalgia, let there be no tears for the passing of the Coliseum. It belonged to another era. And it was never a place for tears, except through laughter.

Gingerbread Castle and Bomb Proof Shelter

If ever St. Paul were subjected to a rain of enemy bombs, I would, if I could get there, hide myself into the impregnable stone block basement of the Angus hotel, that gingerbread castle rising five stories at Selby and Western.

And while the terror swirled about all around, I might pass the time by playing the old 1906 "victrola" still in one cubbyhole of the basement dungeon, or study the Saratoga trunks and old paintings mouldering in the "unclaimed baggage" room.

There would be no danger of collapse from above or the side. Because the Angus, built in 1887, was designed to last, and, having lasted for 71 years and looking toward another hearty 71, it will be a safe harbor.

There are few hotels like the Angus left in these United States, hostelries which retain their aristocratic Victorian gentility, no matter how many coats of pastel paint go on the walls or how modern the furnishings in the rooms.

It wears the same prim, haughty look, exudes the same romance and intrigue and high fashion that it did in 1900 when handsome people and hansom cabs converged on the two entrances at all hours of the day and night.

There is no way and no reason to camouflage the ornate entries, with their grooved stone steps, the colored glass doorpanes, the parquet-tiled floors, nor the desk clerk's inlaid, mahogany counter. Nor the high-ceiling lounges with the pull-out doors, the fireplaces in the rooms and the big bay windows that look out on Selby where the Angus' nobility peers down at the serfs below.

And the stories the place could tell, lurking in the hallway puzzles on every floor where you get lost in broad daylight.

Take all of these away and you wouldn't have the Angus anymore and its guests, many of whom are as distinguished as the building, would probably follow the last piece of fresco ceiling trim right out the door.

But we were down in the cellar, a labyrinth of rooms and halls, created by stone block walls so thick and solid that you feel as if the place were carved out of solid rock.

And the "unclaimed baggage" room. Here is romance and history. Baggage left over the last half century by guests who died, failed to settle a bill or left the hotel "traveling light."

That old Saratoga trunk, with its rounded lid; a vacuum cleaner set of attachments; a suitcase of clothes; an empty strongbox, and paintings, stacked up, facing the walls. The oil paint is cracked in some places, the color tones have darkened on other canvases.

Much of it was done by some long-ago residents who painted in their rooms.

There are old bedsteads that George Washington could have slept in, and chiffoniers dating back that far, it seems. And somebody left a reducing machine, too.

In the boiler room is one unit with "1887" on the firebox. Still holding like the rock of Gibraltar.

Judges, bankers, socialites, retired school teachers, widows with some means, and a flow of transient traders have lived in the Angus. And still do. Names like Scandrett, Bryant, Bingham, Sanborn have been on the register.

"This place was," an Angus resident since 1917 tells me, "born the Albion hotel. It was named the Angus in 1904. Thomas Lowry bought it then."

The same Tom Lowry of Minneapolis fame, the father of the streetcars in the Twin Cities.

"The place hadn't paid very well," she says. "And he decided to change the name. He persuaded Mrs. Messner who ran the Ashland boarding house to come over and run the kitchen and handle other affairs.

"Then, because there were the letters 'A' on the windows already and because he had holdings in a mine called the Angus, I guess he decided to name the hotel Angus. And that's how it got its present name."

In its gala youth, the Angus catered to two dining rooms, three meals a day, for which one paid exactly a dollar.

"And, oh the food on those tables," my informant continues. "Of course, we never dressed for dinner."

There have been deaths and drama and even fires in the Angus' career. But the fireproofing never let a blaze get out of hand.

"I remember one night when a socialite fellow had the room next to ours. He was on a dope jag, and he set his bed on fire. Then he accidentally knocked the telephone off the hook and the night-man came up to see what was wrong. He grabbed the blazing mattress and threw it out the window. It landed right on Selby Avenue."

When the new owners took over the Angus several years ago, the place was astir for a few days, the permanent residents worrying and wondering what would become of it.

Then a cleanup, paintup, modernizing of furnishings began. But the glamor of the old landmark is left intact. And so is the old landmark.

[*Known originally as the Blair Apartment Building, the Angus is now called the Blair Arcade.*]

The Oldest 9th Green in American Golf

It is usually in early or mid-April that the annual surge begins to the city's golf courses where, for the next months, a brave army of men and women chase a little white pill over the hill.

And the air is full of divots and language that casts a blue pall over the fairways, roughs and occasionally the greens.

That time of the year is nigh when numerous matrons look forward to another season of golf widowhood and others, who long ago learned "if you can't fight it, join it," traipse doggedly from bunker to bunker.

Among the many wonderful lies that will be told at the 19th hole and among the many unusual claims, none, I suppose, will delve into one that seems most unusual.

Namely, that St. Paul has the oldest golf club in the United States and the second oldest links continuously played on. BOTH THESE CLAIMS ARE TRUE.

You have but to drive out to Town and Country club on the banks of the Mississippi and Marshall Avenue. to see for yourself this birthplace of golf in St. Paul and Minnesota.

And while John Reid may be the "Father of golf" in America, dating back to 1888 and St. Andrews, near Hastings-on-Hudson, it was an irresponsible *Dispatch* reporter named Charles Hawkes who started it all here.

It was his task, in 1893, to fill a half column twice a week with social notes. And in June of that year he blew into the office of William F. Peet, hunting for news.

Now Mr. Peet was at that time associated with a group who had, in 1888, organized the Town and Country club "for the purpose of social enjoyment and culture" and were at that time operating it as a bicycle club on the banks of the river.

On that historic day, Mr. Peet suggested to Mr. Hawkes that the latter might write a story about the game of golf, which was being talked about out east.

As Mr. Peet tells it, "neither he nor I knew anything about it and as he was too lazy to consult the encyclopedia or any authentic source, he contented himself with the untruthful announcement that I proposed starting the game at the Country Club."

(St. Paul newspaper reporters have since assumed airs of much greater integrity, perhaps thwarting progress as a result.)

On the day after this bombshell burst over the city, the late George McCree, an import from Scotland, went to Mr. Peet and offered to help him start the golf ball rolling.

Mr. Peet decided to give it a try and so, a few days later, loaded a lawnmower and Mr. McCree into the back of his carriage runabout and drove to the club.

"With the assistance of the yard man, we cut the grass on the first green ever used for the game of golf west of New Jersey," Mr. Peet reported.

That green became the ninth when Mr. McCree finished laying out the other eight.

And so golf came to St. Paul and Minnesota and the territory west of the Hudson.

But Mr. Peet's claim to historic fame for golf in St. Paul is based upon the fact that there is only one other links in the nation, older in continuous service, Shinnecock Hills, near Southampton, Long Island.

This was incorporated in 1891. THREE YEARS AFTER the St. Paul group organized as a Country club.

And thus does Mr. Peet, in his records, reason that St. Paul is rightfully the locale of the oldest golf club in the country.

But this will be a bitter pill to swallow for those golf heroes and heroines east of the Alleghenies who still imagine that the only clubs wielded out here are still carried by the Indians.

City Potpourri "The Least of These . . ."

The sign on the front door of the St. Joseph's Children's home says: "Ring the bell and walk in."

And when you cross the threshold of that red stone building at 1458 Randolph, it is a little like walking into the shoe of the woman who had so many children she didn't know what to do.

A few minutes later, Sister Charita, the superintendent, and Sister Alan, the business manager, are saying that they sometimes feel like the "Old Woman," Sister Charita especially on the day recently when she went over and registered her 67 boys and girls for school.

It's just after 3:30 p.m. on this day. And most of the youngsters, 5 to 14, are busy down in the garden, digging potatoes.

But not all of them.

Down the hall come two girlish sprites, Diane and Mary, 5-year-olds, whose bubbling mirth and selves spill over onto the couch and into Sister Charita's arms.

"Have you got any keys?" they shout at me. Then they grab my hands, put their arms around my legs and start dragging me toward the door.

"Let's dig potatoes," they shriek.

That's the way it began—my stay at St. Joseph's.

For the next four hours I lived with those children, a few orphans, most of them from broken homes, or whose mothers or fathers are missing from the family group.

Children, some who had known beatings and been locked up in closets while their parents went out gallivanting through the saloons. So, for a while after they came to St. Joseph's, they still cried when the lights were turned off.

I dug potatoes and petted their ponies; I was grabbed and dragged, by their childish enthusiasm, into every nook and cranny of that building.

I ate supper and even prayed with them in the bright little chapel. I was mightily impressed with Bill, the quarterback of the football team, who knew by memory the words to all the songs that were sung and the ritual that was said.

And the sight of those 67 children, singing lustily, the little girls in clean dresses and wearing hats with ribbons, is something you don't forget when it ends.

There was time, too, for me to peer over their shoulders at study hour, to watch a seventh-grade boy trying to spell "reasonable" while his fingers itched to get at the book at his elbow which was the story of what it takes to be an aviation cadet.

Up in the boys' dormitory I watched them "wash up" for the night, Sister Benedict, looking as stern as she can (which isn't very stern), sleeves rolled up, wielding the wash cloth on the littlest fellows and supervising the cleaning of faces, ears and necks of the rest.

The same Sister Benedict who, an hour or so later after study time, can be observed in the kitchen, filling a pan full of apples to take up to the boys for a late snack before bedtime.

It was up in the dormitory that I met Jackie, a mite with freckles, hardly 5. He wanted to show me the bed which the boys had made for me (they had hoped I would spend the night with them) and there was a great big teddy bear on the pillow.

"Where did you get that?" I said.

One of the older boys replied:

"Aw, one of the guys won it at the State Fair throwing baseballs." Because they go to bed earlier than the rest, Jackie and the other two youngest boys have their own room. But Jackie wanted to show me how he rides "Black Beauty." So he galloped down the floor between the rows of beds, slapping his side, right into Sister Charita, who picked him up on the fly.

As he ran back for another demonstration, Sister looked after him and then she said:

"His parents certainly are missing something, aren't they?"

This was Thursday night and everybody was trying hard to be good. Because Friday afternoon the children can leave for the weekend if they have a place to visit.

But, discipline being a necessity, those who falter in school or behavior sometimes do not have that week-end privilege.

There was Rudy, for instance.

"He is being awfully good," said Sister Charita. "He couldn't go last weekend."

And Rudy came up then to report that he was an altar boy, as of last Monday, when he served his first mass.

Then he went back to change the sheets on his bed and nobody can make a hospital corner like Rudy. He'd pass the toughest West Point inspection with a commendation.

But there are others I must mention, too.

Timmy. He had only been there three weeks. And his eighth birthday had been a few days earlier. It was just before supper that Sister Charita handed me an envelope. "A women's organization gives each child a card and two dollars on his or her birthday," she said. "This is Timmy's. He has been lonesome here. Will you give it to him?"

So I did. And Timmy's smile never left his face the rest of that night—after he'd done waving those two dollar bills around the dining room.

And I should tell you, too, about the two little girls who wanted me to carry them so they could rub their faces against my chin whiskers—which sent them into gales of giggles.

Nor will I forget Marlene, who is 5, and gives everybody a big kiss, which she immediately wipes off your face.

"You look like Davy Crockett's friend," she told me soberly. I wish I could have stayed longer—until Halloween, as Mary wanted me to, so "you can carve a jack-o-lantern. And you can eat at our table and I'll give you some of my allowance to buy candy and pop with." (All the children get an allowance.)

Sister Charita walked to the door with me when I left.

"The people of St. Paul have been awfully kind to us," she said. (The home is a Community Chest agency.) "And the children here have some advantage of companionship that other youngsters might not have. And learn things that others may not learn.

"But they all miss something that we cannot provide."

And she was looking across the lawn towards the homes of the city and their friendly lights.

Did You Ever Go to Jefferson School?

If, some day, you happen to be in Rome, Stockholm, Paris, along the upper Nile or in Hong Kong, stop the first American who passes and ask:

"Did you ever go to Jefferson school at St. Paul?"

And the chances are more than middling good that the answer will be: "Yes."

Because, while other schools have shared the peak of fame, has there ever been one in the city, or any city, whose graduates have penetrated so widely into the world's hemispheres as old Jefferson—which once stood in the vicinity of Pleasant and Sherman?

The bonds which tie old Jeff alumni are stronger than most. So that when two persons meet, a lodge card, letter of credit, or the old fraternity handshake have pale influence compared with evidence of a diploma from the school.

There was, for instance, the Paris incident in 1947 when Mrs. Olivia Johnson, on a visit there, became displeased with the food at her hotel and, looking down the street, spotted a U. S. Army mess.

"That," she said, "is where I will eat." But, regulations and all, she could not gain admittance. A determined woman, she tried nonetheless and made the rounds of the military offices, looking for an Open Sesame to the food line.

She would never have found the key had it not been for a certain Col. William A. Mann who recognized her, after 40 years or more, as a schoolmate from Jefferson.

Such has been the prestige of Jefferson school.

Among some once-Jeffersonians are Gen. Matt Ridgway and his sister, Ruth, and Gen. Follett Bradley. There was Blanche Yurka, Broadway star still active on the stage, and Graham MacNamee.

And Beatrice Pleiss, who later married Sarah Bernhardt's publicity man and toured the world with the actress.

And, locally, Municipal Judge Archie L. Gingold and Assistant School Superintendent John Gran.

Also a concentration of famous St. Paul names, among them, Waterous, Nelson, Shearan, Lilly, Ryan, Garrity, Kelly, Shiely, Van Hoven, Holm, Ohage, Zimmerman, Groff, Defiel and O'Brien. Also Mrs. Royal Dow and Mrs. Katherine Scott. And others whom it is best not to mention, whose notoriety eventually took them to prison cells.

At this point, the logical question is what did Jefferson have that the other schools didn't?

It was built in 1858 and dedicated in the fall, a rather elegant structure, facing Pleasant. It was, according to the best recollection of Otto Rohland Sr., a white frame building, located about where Children's hospital now stands.

A fire in 1866 destroyed the building, fortunately in June after classes were out. And another Jefferson was built at Pleasant and Sherman.

An addition was made in 1877 and there it stood, gray brick and stone sides turning grimy, until 1927. It was torn down, finally, or did it totter down?

John Gran recalls that in its last years, the school's top floor students were not permitted to march out to recess, to the beat of a triangle, for fear the weaving old steps would collapse.

In the beginning, when the Seven Corners area and the Hill district were the finest residential sections, the children of the elite went to Jefferson. And, gradually, as the area changed into the more commonplace neighborhoods, the student body shifted in background. Thus the wide variety of faces and intellects.

In the era when Fort Snelling was a busy Army post and schools were scarce, children of the soldiers were driven to Jefferson school each morning, in a canvas-topped, horse-drawn wagon, managed by Bernard Cobeny. And in winter-time, the wheels were replaced by a sleigh.

Mrs. Amy Birdsall, editor of the Women's department of the St. Paul papers, rode in from the Fort each day with the Ridgways, the youngsters carrying cold lunches and scraping their feet on the straw to keep warm.

In the hierarchy of Jefferson school, there are faculty names that will excite the memories of thousands.

H. S. Baker, the principal, whose massive feet required that he take the steps sideways and who was looked up to with awe by his little chargelings, who regarded him as a great protector.

And also, Nellie O'Keefe, a principal in later years; not to forget also, Lillian McGuire, Miss Mary O'Brien, Nellie Baker, Maud and Kit Clum, Emma and Sophie Witt. And a certain Prof. Dahle, who came down to direct musicals on "Red Letter day" occasions.

In one such affair, Blanche Yurka played the role of "King of the Land of Nod," though it is not recorded among such other of her successes as "I Remember Mama."

And who can forget Arbor day at Jefferson, when the cherubs marched up Oakland hill and planted plum and apple trees that are still growing on the slopes—or at least their off-shoots are?

Or the spelling bees on Friday afternoons?

For sport, there was always the old streetcar barn nearby where the young blades would delight in purloining bells. And later, in the barn behind the school—now an education department shop—there were major wars between the Rice Street and the West Side gangs.

These were during recess, when a lookout was posted to watch for the "law" and the cry, "Jiggers, here comes the principal," sent a shiver through combatants and spectators alike.

Those were the days when, in the male social system, prominence was based upon "Who can you lick?" and the names at the top were constantly changing.

It was a half century of education, some part of which is instantly recalled, when someone who "lived over the hill" meets somebody who "lived under the hill" on a street corner in a distant land.

Of Faith and Belief

Cathedral's New Bells Will Ring with History

As the rector of the Cathedral of St. Paul, Monsignor Ambrose Hayden plays a variety of parts: pastor, counselor, special activities scheduling clerk, tour guide, emergency heating engineer and shepherd of a parish flock.

Just lately, he has also become an author of a continuing serial called "The Cathedral Bells," which has appeared chapter by chapter in the parish's Sunday bulletins since early September.

It is the continuing tale of five swinging bronze bells weighing a combined 17,515 pounds. They are being cast and created in southern France to go into the south tower of the Cathedral next year.

Believe it or not, this quintet will be the Cathedral's very first bells of status and stature. As Hayden says, "The little, lone bell we now have in the north tower, which rang from (the former) Cathedral at Sixth and St. Peter streets, couldn't scare the pigeons away."

In the first chapter of the Gospel of the Bells according to Hayden, the readers and worshippers were told that the five bells are now being cast by the Paccard-Fonderie de Cloches of Annecy, France, and that the largest bell will weigh 6,600 pounds and the smallest 1,545 pounds. (This is the same firm which has installed bells up Summit Avenue at House of Hope Presbyterian church.)

The Cathedral of St. Paul by Julie Hiebert

The bells, each tuned to a note on the musical scale, will ring out the Angelus three times a day, toll for funerals, ring joyously for weddings and other major religious holidays, as well as "being on call for special civic functions."

To blunt any residential qualms, Hayden also wrote, "Neighbors, have no fear, we shall not interrupt your sleep! Discretion will prevail."

One entire chapter has been devoted to the naming of the bells, after saints, according to a practice dating to 756.

A great deal of Minnesota and church history has been used by Hayden in choosing the names.

The largest bell will, of course, be called St. Paul, apostle to the Gentiles and patron of the archdiocese. Inscribed on the bell will be a quotation from one of Paul's Epistles to the Romans: "Their voice has sounded over all the Earth" and, in this case at least, as far as Minneapolis.

The second bell will be Mary's bell (the Blessed Virgin), and the daily Angelus will be rung on it.

The third bell will bear the names of the Archangels, Sts. Michael, Gabriel and Raphael.

"We'll turn to a little history, too, to show another reason for their choice," Hayden wrote in the Oct. 6 chapter.

The first Mass celebrated in Minnesota was on Nov. 4, 1727, at Fort Beauharnois near Old Frontenac, where the little chapel was named St. Michael. The founder and first pastor of our Cathedral parish, Lucian Galtier, spent his last years as pastor of the Church of St. Gabriel in Prairie du Chien, Wisconsin, where he is buried near the front entrance. The Cathedral at Dubuque, Iowa, the diocese from which we arose in 1850, is named St. Raphael. When that bell rings, it will recall a lot of history.

The fourth bell will recall the first canonized North American saint, St. Frances (Mother) Xavier Cabrini, who ministered to the poor and the immigrants, especially the Italians.

The last bell will honor St. John Vianney, secondary patron of the Cathedral, better known as the Curé of Ars, France, and popular among Minnesota Catholics.

There is a strong Minnesota connection to Vianney. He was well-known to Bishop Cretin, who sent two young priests, John Ireland and Thomas O'Gorman, to Ars to meet the famed priest. Cretin knew of the huge crowds that swarmed around the curé, and so he told the two young priests to push through the crowd and shout: "Bishop Cretin sent us!" They did, and Vianney took them to his house for a meeting, his blessing and gave them some medals.

The question is always asked, "Why has there been only one puny, little bell in the Cathedral's north tower for so many years?"

"I'll explain it to you," the Cathedral pastor told me the other day when we discussed the bells.

"That original little bell was used to keep John Ireland on schedule. When it was moved to the Cathedral up here, he couldn't hear it, so the pastor, Lawrence O'Brien, told me he had to keep the Archbishop on time vocally.

"I'm sure it was on John Ireland's mind and in the minds of many others to someday fill that musical gap. But there were always other priorities until now."

Nowhere in any of his chapters does Hayden mention the cost of the bells. And his pitches for funds have been soft or non-existent.

"I don't have to," he smiles. "The funds will be there."

Hayden may already have written his last paragraph, a quotation from the *Catholic Bulletin* newspaper in 1904 about the planned construction of the new Cathedral:

"When future generations will go up to this monument of faith, this house of the Lord, exalted above the hills, they will admire and bless the spirit that animated their forefathers in the ancient faith to do such great, magnanimous things for God.

"To crown this work, a peal of five swinging bronze bells."

A monument, too, to Monsignor Ambrose Hayden.

Silent Sentinel; Guardian of the City's Morals

It was a raw, gloomy afternoon, windy and hinting of sleet, when I trudged up to the Cathedral to check a report that this towering edifice was at last, after 48 years, nearing completion.

During the laborious climb up the long hill in the shadow of the Cathedral's granite majesty, I thought that even the most seasoned of world travelers might indeed catch some of the feeling of awe that the mighty structure inspires when you approach it from the front on foot.

For a few minutes before I went into the Cathedral itself, I chatted with the rector and our guide, Monsignor George E. Ryan. And to talk to him about the Cathedral is a rare experience because of his ready wit, easy smile and vast knowledge of Cathedral lore.

"Yes," he said, "with our present plans, the Cathedral—the heart of it—will be finished within the next year. The fabric will be completed.

"With us," he added, "it has been like the owner of a home of which he is proud. We add a little here and there."

Within a few days, one more step will be taken. A giant chandelier will be hoisted into the dome. It will be shaped like an eight-pointed star and light from each point will illuminate the eight bays in the dome. The star will be 12 feet in diameter and hang 96 feet from the ceiling. But that will still be 90 feet above the floor, Father Ryan said.

"Then we have a few pieces of sculpture to add and a stained glass window is in the process of being finished. And that will about do it, I believe."

But even as it stands now, the Cathedral is one of the nation's three greatest—the other two being St. Patrick's in New York City and St. Louis Cathedral, which isn't anywhere near finished. In fact, said Father Ryan, the architects from there were in St. Paul not long ago studying the Cathedral for ideas.

And Father Ryan reminded me of what Cass Gilbert, architect for the State Capitol, once said when he viewed the two domes— the Capitol and the Cathedral.

"If this city, with those monumental structures, were moved to Europe, St. Paul would be one of the historic show places of the old world."

I walked over to the Cathedral from Father Ryan's office and a rush of cold wind knifed past us as we opened a door and stepped inside. And then, suddenly, it was calm and silent, the turmoil of the city around and below the Cathedral, shut out by the door closing on the latch. The atmosphere was filled with the scent of delicate perfumes.

We stood for a moment on the threshold of the interior, looking through dim light across the rows of pews which seat 4,000 worshippers. Two women knelt in prayer and another sat in meditation. Far back, a man walked in, paused and sat down.

While Father Ryan went to turn up the lights, I looked to the center of the dome, then at the far walls. An optical illusion has been created by the harmonious carrying out of architectural perspective. The Cathedral, vast as it is, seems small and comfortable. An oval, stained-glass window may appear to be only about 6 feet in diameter when in reality it is 30 feet.

Father Ryan returned and, pointing to the ceiling, showed me where the new chandelier would go. A single light bulb now hangs there.

As I walked into the ambulatory which skirts the Cathedral apse, Father Ryan nodded toward a base for a piece of sculpture.

"Place for one of those pieces of sculpture I mentioned," he said.

Along the passageway to the left of the throne, we stopped to see the six chapels called the Shrines of the Nations, in which are statues of the patron saints of the nations whose people settled St. Paul.

At each shrine is some work in marble, imported from the particular country so honored.

Father Ryan stepped over to the seven bronze grilles between the piers back of the altar. Full-sized figures which form the frieze in the grilles are done in three dimensions.

He opened a door in one of the grilles. "Try it and see how heavy it is—solid bronze," he said. I did and it took stern effort.

The lights were beginning to come on in the downtown district at the foot of the Cathedral when I left Father Ryan.

I looked back once or twice and above the great arch of the main doorway, we saw the figure of Christ and the Apostles grouped around, watching the city in stolid silence.

The vision of the beloved Archbishop John Ireland, who decided to put the Cathedral on that commanding site, was nearing final fruition, I thought.

And I remembered Father Ryan's words:

"If you write something, tell the people who will move into the approach after the redevelopment program is finished that they will find a beautiful new church waiting for them."

Potatoes and Hymns on Jackson Street

You can pass a building day after day, year after year, and do nothing more than rest your eyes on it. And in the press of traffic, forging back and forth along Jackson, many have less than a casual glance for the big, solid, stone and brick structure with the faded look that stands on the northwest corner.

Then one day somebody piques your interest. You go up Jackson and look at it squarely and the old building registers.

"That peaked roof? It seems to be a clue."

But in modesty, lacking the fine, fresh finish of the newer Loop buildings and the glass block walls and chrome, the old building offers only that slim hint of a story.

Ah, but it could wear its exterior with pride and grandeur— standing haughtily alongside these young pups of modern architecture, who may never know half the history of 157-59 E. Ninth at Jackson.

For this building, on the edge of the market district, is one of the less than a handful still standing after a century. Built in 1856, it was.

Not only is it 102 years old, but for that entire span it has contributed to the welfare of the city—first as a place of worship, then as an economic force. It has never been long without tenants.

This was the second Methodist church in the city, Jackson Street M. E. church, they called it. And its congregation was part of the first Methodist church society in St. Paul.

The original—the first—Methodist church in the brawling, infant village was the Market Street M. E. church, which stood facing Rice Park on the present site of the Hotel St. Paul parking lot.

Rapidly outgrowing its size, the congregation built the Jackson Street church, figuring to move en masse. But only part of them did—in 1856. The rest stayed up on Market. Then in 1857 they tried uniting there on Jackson, but separated a year later.

Thus half the first Methodist congregation made Jackson Street church their "house of worship." The others formed First Methodist church.

And to this day, both congregations claim to be descendants of the original. And both are correct.

Edward Eggleston, who later became one of the nation's foremost authors and wrote *The Hoosier Schoolmaster* and *Circuit Rider* preached there for two years.

And in 1862, after the Indian battle at Birch Coulee, 12 parishioners of Jackson Street M. E. church were buried from the church—each a victim of the massacre.

And though they may have deplored undo concentration on material wealth, the mortgage was a constant harassment.

Jackson Street church was built for $16,000 (it has been sold for many times that amount since) but the parishioners had to take on a $9,000 mortgage.

Just as foreclosure seemed imminent, the church added to its roster of trustees the names of B. F. Hoyt and J. C. Quinby. And with outside contributions from Christians in the city, the mortgage was paid off in full. In the celebration of thanksgiving and gratitude that followed, 70 persons were converted to the faith in one night.

"A glorious revival," says a brief footnote to the church history.

And in 1887—after selling the church building to E. Longevin for $35,000—the congregation left Jackson Street forever and moved up a few blocks to a new home and new name—Central Park Methodist Church, at 12th and Minnesota.

If its stature had been mightily diminished, the old building at least has had a varied career since.

At one time a spice dealer located there. And in 1933, for instance, it was the Libman Auction mart.

Gradually the city moved away—toward the river, toward the hills, on the plateaus and No. 157-59 was part of the market district.

These days, it is being used by the Dege Seed Co. and Tom Colenso's wholesale vegetable business. They have been there 18 years now.

And Tom, standing in the back room packaging potatoes, recalled the day a man about 80 walked in, looked around a little and when asked what he wanted, replied:

"Oh, nothing, really. I just thought I'd come down and look at the place where I was baptized."

And his voice was nearly drowned out by the hymn—of commerce—as the potato packaging machine roared to a crescendo, showing off rafters that once rang with praise of God in the wilderness of Ninth and Jackson.

History of St. Mary's Coming Alive

The first time I met her was in the fusty, dusty attic of old St. Joseph's Academy, and she was cleaning out the archives because the school was closing after 120 years. That was 1971 and Sister Ann Thomasine Sampson and I spent some fascinating hours pouring over records, musing over names written in the ledgers: Mary Mehegan, who became Mrs. James J. Hill; Chippewa Chief Hole-in-the Day, who sent his daughter to the school; then the daughters of a fellow named Ireland, one of whom became Mother Seraphine, the movable spirit behind the College of St. Catherine and the entire order. Names like that.

It was a taste of history that Sister Ann savored, and she lugged most of the old documents, not to mention religious artifacts, to the St. Joseph's Provincial House. She didn't know it then, but after a long career of teaching music, directing the choir, singing and playing, the closing of old SJA was the opening of her second career—unless you count her avocation: apostolate of touring America and the Great Lakes on river tows and freighters.

The next time I saw her, she was sitting in her basement office in the Provincial House on Randolph Avenue. She'd got a grant of money from the Grotto Foundation and was starting a vast and indepth history project of collecting oral and written histories on every one of the St. Joseph's nuns. That also made her the official spokesperson for the order whenever a nun was in the news. She had every biography on tape and in her files.

She got interviews with some of the Golden Age sisters just in time.

But nobody else had ever thought of it and her achievements began bringing big recognition from state, county and national historical groups and agencies.

That fame reached the tundra of Jamestown, North Dakota, where she was asked to do a history of St. John's Academy boarding school.

The next time I saw her, she had finished that and was into a big history of St Agatha's Conservatory at Exchange and Cedar streets, where scores of young men and women learned piano, violin and dance in a civilizing influence on the rough, raw frontier town.

Now she's waded into a huge new history project, writing a book and creating all kinds of other programs and exhibits for the 100th birthday of St. Mary's Hospital in Minneapolis. And that's where I found her the other morning, on the eighth floor of the main building, in a tidy office filled with old ledger books, pictures and diaries.

"This may well be the major historical effort of my life," she said. "The centennial isn't until 1987, but when Sister Rita Clare called me up to discuss it, we agreed it's nice to get started early."

Sister Rita Clare, former administrator and now consultant to the administrator, is herself one of the stars in the hospital's history. The present main building is her monument, along with a lot of the programs that have gone on inside. She has been called the leader, creator and pusher of modern St. Mary's—all of which she eschews in a voice that has a lilt from her native Tipperary.

"We're all very enthusiastic about our centennial. It's going to last all year. Sister Ann's work will be part of all of it."

Sister Ann has gone about her historical research like a candidate running for office. Displaying her name tag that says "historian," she lopes through the hospital cafeteria shaking hands, meeting people, telling them what she is doing and always asking the inevitable question: "If you have any ideas, tips or suggestions about the history, please come up to Room A842."

Every bulletin board has a memo asking for old pictures, bills, awards, diplomas, uniforms, catalogs, ledgers, logos, postcards, banners, clippings, articles, slogans, buttons and symbols.

She has inveigled her way into staff meetings to talk about her efforts.

The seed is being harvested.

"Do you know that we have had Sweetsers on the medical staff since we opened in 1887? There was Dr. Horatio B., his two sons, Horatio Jr. and Theodore Sr. Then there's Dr. Theodore Jr. (he was president of the medical staff) and one of the daughters married into the Preston family, and Dr. Frank Preston will be the new chief of staff in 1984."

Sister Ann pulls out a copy of the very first register of patients, which she found deep in the hospital's recesses.

"We ought to put up a plaque to this fellow," she says, pointing to patient No. 1, James Hannephin's name inscribed in fine Spenserian writing. He was a Canadian, admitted on September 28, 1887, in what had been the old brick mansion owned by Capt. Edward Murphy on the river bluff "right where we still are," says Sister Ann.

"Maybe, though we shouldn't put up a plaque for No. 1. He came in with tuberculosis and died the next spring. We didn't do him much good.

"You know what I learn from reading these rosters? I learn that there was a terrific immigration of people from all over Europe in that period of our beginning and they had the same diseases and ailments we still have, only with other names, *la grippe* for the flu and so on. I read how they had forms of health insurance called 'Sister Tickets' during the depressions of 1893 and '97."

In her file of "VIP Personalities," of course, is Sister Mary Madonna, inspiration for the internationally known St. Mary's Chemical Dependency Treatment Center and Physical-Occupational Therapy Rehab Centers and currently the state health commissioner.

Then there's the famous Rev. Paschal Kelly, the priest with multiple sclerosis who lived almost 30 years at St. Mary's, immobile in bed. He did "miraculous things" without leaving his room, like mending broken marriages, bringing people together, preventing suicides, and, in 1968, securing for my family front-row tickets to Pope Paul VI's Christmas Mass in Rome.

"You're in the VIP file, too," said Sister Ann. "I was saving this for last," she said. "A sort of subtle suggestion you'd want to write about us." She handed me a copy of my own birth record, 12:30 a.m., June 9, 1921.

"Handled like a real public relations pro," I said. "How can I turn you down, except for one small detail?"

"They spelled my name wrong."

Legend of a Head Stone

It has been many a moon since the signal fires of the Chippewa last blazed from the top of the Riverview bluffs overlooking the mighty Father of Waters. The quiet, calm of Riverview cemetery—at the end of Annapolis street—has occupied that high ground in the white man's time.

And yet there, under a modest field stone marker, beneath the shade trees at the side of a road winding through the cemetery, lies a modern Indian legend. It is a story to quicken the pulse of the lover of such lore.

For the old field stone—dwarfed by the ornate and carefully hewn headstones around it—is the resting place of an Indian princess named Seneca and her husband, who was Chief White Cloud.

She was Ahnahneitta and he Pottowatomie and because they lived in the white man's world, they were also Mr. and Mrs. Burton L. Baker.

They lived near Mendota. He was born in 1870 and she in 1875—full-blooded Chippewas. When, in 1930, Princess Seneca died, her chief brought the stone one day and set it at the head of her grave. Carefully he chiseled the inscription.

"Seneca, Princess of White Cloud, Ahnahneitta Baker, B. 1875 D. 1930." And below it he inscribed: "Pottowawatomie, Burton L. Baker, B. 1870."

On the sides he wrote the Chippewa commandments:

"Do not steal, do not lie, be true."

There are Indian symbols, all nearly worn away by the weather.

Seneca's chief remained true to her memory through the years. Gerald Warnke, superintendent of the cemetery, remembers how Baker came in fair weather and foul to visit his princess. And every few years he would chisel out the words anew.

Then one day in February of 1957, Chief White Cloud came back to his princess—to stay.

And so they lie there together, more popular in death than in life because every summer visitors come to see whether the legend is true.

The Beginning of a City Also Is the End

Historians, when they record the story of a city, too often brush lightly over one of the most fascinating phases—the cemeteries.

And yet, show me a city where the cemetery is not perhaps the best place to begin in picking up the threads of those who built the community.

St. Paul's cemetery history is little known, yet the details have as much drama, perhaps, as the other phases of the city's growth.

A touch of this interest is usually aroused when excavators for some building or street suddenly come upon the bones of a long-gone settler, provoking speculation as to whether some hidden cemetery has been uncovered.

And such has been the case here, frequently.

Imagine, for instance, the surprise on the face of William F. Markoe of White Bear Lake in 1856 when, as they were grading St. Peter Street near Summit, he saw the ends of coffins protruding from the banks on both sides of the streets.

What he was seeing was the remains, literally, of the Protestant Episcopal Mission cemetery on the one side, where Park Place now stands, and the second Catholic cemetery on the opposite side of the street.

And in 1910 when the Soo Line tunnel was being built at the head of Olive Street, four or five caskets were found. These were once in what was either the Olive Street or Christ Church cemeteries.

In 1919 a workman dug up three skeletons while excavating at 395 Hatch. What he had got into was old Oak Hill cemetery, bounded by Front, Western, MacKubin and Maryland.

At least one illustrious son was first buried there—James M. Goodhue, editor and founder of the *Pioneer Press*. His story is a bit of irony. It was Goodhue who, in 1852, campaigned for a cemetery at that site.

And, as the story goes, he was one of the first to make use of it. His body later was removed to more suitable quarters in Oakland cemetery.

Back when the newest building at St. Joseph's Academy was being erected at Iglehart and Virginia, builders came upon some bones. And the Mother Superior put in a hasty call to Paul Daggett, director of Catholic cemeteries.

"You'll have to send some men over here right away," she said. "We just found some bodies."

Mr. Daggett dispatched some workmen with a rough box who gathered up the remains and took them to Calvary cemetery where they are recorded only as "X" for the "Unknown quantities."

The mother superior was unaware, I suppose, that the present site of St. Joseph's Academy was once the third Catholic cemetery in the city, from 1853 to 1856, and gave way to Calvary, the Fourth and last in the St. Paul limits.

It won't, probably, spoil anybody's fun at the State Fair to learn that the Poor Farm burial ground once was located near the place where the loop-the-loops and the Midway now entertain the masses.

There is really nothing mysterious or odd about these hidden cemeteries, according to Mr. Daggett, who has made it one of his hobbies to assemble what are possibly the only complete notes on St. Paul cemeteries.

As the city grew, its burial places moved with it, always seeking the edge of the habitation. And, in the course of moving from place to place, it is only natural that a few graves were overlooked.

Not so much from carelessness. But because early locating systems were somewhat informal and haphazard.

You could record, for instance, that so-and-so's grave was five feet east from a grove of trees. But how are you going to find it years later when the trees have been cut down?

And so a few odds and ends keep turning up and may for many years to come as the city's structure changes.

I have, so far, mentioned the Second, Third and Fourth Catholic cemeteries and some of the Protestant or nondenominational. To get things into their historical perspective, one should go back to the beginning of cemeteries here. And that is the First Catholic cemetery, which was the first burial plot in the city.

You will find that, if you look some day, about where the parking lot behind the *Dispatch* and *Pioneer Press* pressroom now stands. On the west corner of Minnesota and Kellogg Boulevard.

And that spot seems reasonable when you remember that Rev. Lucian Galtier erected the first log chapel on adjoining property and the churchyard quite naturally became the cemetery.

For the record, the first burial known to have been made in St. Paul, in the churchyard plot, was that of Cecile LaBissoniere, who died Aug. 22, 1841.

The first undertaker in Minnesota was a Capt. Washington M. Stees, who also ran a furniture store not far from the cemetery, which made it quite handy.

In his historical diggings on the subject, Mr. Daggett has occasionally turned up some interesting items in addition to the remains of the city's deceased pioneers.

For example, he found that St. Paul has had its own quadruplets, born April 1, 1876, to Archibald McDonald and wife. The first baby was stillborn, the second lived a month and the other two four months. They are buried in Calvary cemetery.

Because as has happened in the past, some almost forgotten, uncharted cemeteries have been discovered, it is not certain that every locale has been bench-marked.

And it isn't too far out of the realm of possibility to say that wherever you live in the city, you can never be sure someone else hasn't rested there earlier.

Country School on Tenth Street

Just around the corner on Tenth, off Cedar, at the edge of the St. Paul Loop, the song of "Alouette" still rings out on happy young voices against the raucous city symphony.

And if those, in the hurry of life, pause to listen, they may find themselves gazing up at the little-domed building which is the source of this song. Then they may read the words imprinted over the door: "Ecole St. Louis—St. Louis School," which in the parlance of time has come to be known as "The Little French School" of St. Louis Catholic church. Not like any other school in the city.

It is a little building, trimmed at the eaves and made more intriguing because it is hidden so shyly against the loftier pillars of concrete, the sterner buildings of the blocks around.

But, if you have an hour to spend some afternoon, before the hour of 3, it will be worth your while to peek in at busy business inside, where—in grades 1 through 8—second and sometimes third-generation children of French parents recite and learn. In the same four rooms, their mothers and fathers, grandfathers and grandmothers sat doing the same thing.

Yet because this is the melting pot, these days the Le Vasseurs, Goyettes and Juaires—who come from miles away—sit with other youngsters of all nationalities—Italian, German, Black, Oriental and Spanish. They all live on the Loop's fringe.

And because the French influence has faded with Americanization, it is only in their songs that you will hear French which was taught as a subject as late as the 1930s.

The exterior charm of St. Louis school is an alluring cover for more inside. As you go up the stone steps, hollowed by children's feet since 1886, you mentally review the past of Ecole St. Louis, established there in a frame building in 1873, on land donated by Bishop Grace, as a French school for French Catholics who pioneered the city.

The building is flush with the sidewalk and the fenced-in playground, at the rear, tiny by comparison to most, looks down into the heart of the city. Yet, when you step inside St. Louis school, you feel atmosphere, of a little family of students and four teachers, three of them nuns. It is like walking into a pleasant land of learning, an island of imagination, unfettered dreams and ambitions. Set in the mood of the old country school in the wilderness, flavored by the still evident French culture that will never leave St. Louis school.

And the surrounding city hardly knows it's there.

There is no hallway at St. Louis. Just a small foyer and two sets of stairs winding steeply up either side to the second floor where Sister Paul Mary, the principal and 7th and 8th grade teacher, waits with a smile.

"Welcome to the little French school," she says. And she has set the tenor of the visit. Hard to describe. How, in each of the four classrooms, the students rose in a welcome, en masse. And one by one they introduced themselves as daughters and sons of parents who had also attended St. Louis.

In Sister Christino's 5th and 6th grade room, Ronald Holly spoke about the French school and Julia Taube, not at all French, led eight verses of "Alouette." And Sister Severina's little 1st and 2nd graders sang a song, welcoming me to their school, one they undoubtedly had spent industrious hours learning.

I have never been paid a finer nor more sincere honor.

And in Miss Bernadette Murray's 3rd and 4th grade they proudly presented me with a copy of my book to autograph for them.

In between I got what Sister Paul Mary described as the "$2.50 tour." As we climbed to the third floor, she told how the Sisters of St. Joseph of Carondelet had been specially assigned to open St. Louis school because they spoke French in the early days. "Now, I doubt that any of us could do a creditable job," she says.

The old auditorium, on the third floor, once the scene of plays and programs, is empty from disuse, cold and forlorn-looking. But neat and clean as a hospital room. The window of the box office at the back is boarded shut and on the stage under the archway stand boxes of clothes.

"Some of our children need these," says Sister Paul Mary. "We haven't used the auditorium for years. But it must have been a happy place when we had big enrollments. It was a classroom, too. Now we have only 131 students. A League of Nations with French overtones."

In that first class of 1873 there were just 130 students. With names like Auge, Gadbois, LaPointe, Nadeau, LaMarre, Vaillancourt, Souci—and, by the way, two named O'Toole and Kelly.

I learned that of all "St. Louis" families, the Lancettes graduated the most persons, but nobody knows exactly how many. And I heard, too, about an almost legendary sister, Octavia, who petitioned to come to St. Louis school from Canada because she thought only French was spoken and she spoke no English. She remained for several decades, now lives in retirement at Bethany home.

"There are some disadvantages in being surrounded by the city's business and industry," says Sister Paul Mary. "But look how close we are to places to go on field trips—the Public Safety building, a half block away, the Capitol up the street, the Historical society. We are in the center of things we study. Nobody is luckier."

[Ecole St. Louis is now a parking lot for St. Louis Church.]

H Stands for Heaven

I don't usually dedicate a column to anyone. But this is for Vic. He lives in Canada and I only met him once, may never see him again.

But he wants me to send him a copy of this column so he can keep it in his wallet and read it some days when his morale is down and thoughts of faltering enter his mind.

Vic can't afford to falter. Not in the way I mean. Vic is an alco-holic. And what I am reminding him about is the story I am telling you—of a place called Miracle House. Only in the brochures and on the sign just off Highway 8 near Center City it's called Hazelden. Some say the H stands for Heaven instead of Hazelden.

I spent a day at this amazing place which, since 1948, has reha-bilitated some 1,700 alcoholics from among men you know or meet on the street.

Not the skid row D-horns, not the down-and-outers. But bankers, lawyers, doctors, salesmen, corporation presidents, educators, clergy-men. These are men with responsibilities, families, intellect and talent. And they were—were, I say—alcoholics, racked by a strange disease which, defying the people to explain, has wrongfully been given a stigma more degrading and loathsome than the Salem witchcrafters.

I talked with them, ate with them and roamed the 180 acres of rolling bright green grass and shrubs, which sweep around a sky blue lake where they sit in the sun and get tan and read the books and meditate and talk to each other about their sickness and swap their alibis for drinking until at last they start thinking about the long way back and take the first steps.

You don't "dry out" or take "the cure" at Hazelden. You learn and think and study and rest, watch TV, wash your own clothes, help with the dishes, savor the juicy steaks and pray hard.

And having recognized, at last, that "the good Lord helps those who also help themselves," you get up off your back and do it.

So here is where I met Vic. But I met some others, too:

There is Bud who drove me out to Hazelden. Bud is 40 and he is an alcoholic. This trim, alert man?

"I saw the world through an alcoholic fog," he says. "Bartenders used to groan when they saw me coming. I was drinking hair tonic and burned out my mouth with liquor.

"Then one day I went on an awful drunk in Chicago and woke up in the Hotel Lowry in St. Paul. Next thing I knew a man from

Alcoholics Anonymous picked me up and I spent a few days at Hazelden's St. Paul clubrooms. They gave me a job. That was 28 months ago.

"I'm glad I'm an alcoholic. Because now I can appreciate things I never saw before. The green fields over there, the sunshine, the little things along the road, good food, and sleep."

At lunch that noon I sat with a couple and their 10-year-old daughter. They come from Iowa. For them it was an anniversary. The man had been flown to Hazelden on July 4 a year ago by a friend who owned a plane.

"I remember drinking my last beer on the plane, then threatening to toss the bottle over the side," he said.

He spent a month at Hazelden (three weeks is the minimum) and now he was back in triumph, with his wife and daughter. They were staying in a guest cabin, near the main house, which is reserved for "old grads" who like to bring their families back on anniversaries.

Upstairs in the walnut-paneled quarters of Lynn Carroll, the director, a few minutes later, the man from Iowa came to say goodbye.

Then Mr. Carroll turned and told about Hazelden and the parade of names and faces that have passed through the halls of the spacious residence.

"You laugh and you cry with them," he says. "And you admire each one.

"I guess I have heard every alibi for alcoholism there is," he went on.

"You want a funny one? Well, there was one man whose family had raised some geese. One day they decided to sell them to a butcher, so the man took them to the shop. Just as he was leaving, one of those geese looked at him with such a woebegone expression that it bothered him as he started home.

"Suddenly he turned, went back to get that goose, but he was too late. It had been butchered. And that," says Mr. Carroll, "is the reason he gave for going on a drunk.

"Hazelden," he said, "to give you vital statistics, was founded in 1948 by a group of St. Paul and Minneapolis civic leaders, (Patrick Butler is president of the foundation), who thought something should be done for the alcoholic. It is a private, non-profit institution and it will cost you $300 for three weeks. There aren't many in the country like it.

"The only people we want to help are those where alcohol has become a problem in handling their daily affairs.

"I call it an illness. Do you know any man in his right mind who would willingly degrade himself, his family, lose his job and become known as the town's 'lush'?"

At Hazelden, the road back doesn't end with the farewells. And so we come back to Vic. He was leaving that day. He rode back to St. Paul with us. Before he left, Mr. Carroll and he had a last conference, charting Vic's course.

As we drove into the city, Vic looked out at the scenery. He was a little nervous.

"I used to get drunk on Wednesdays and stay drunk until Monday. The kids—I've got three—would wait for me every night and I'd be at some bar. God knows I wanted to be home, but I couldn't.

"Four weeks ago a friend told me about Hazelden. I got on a plane and came. I very nearly slipped in New York City, but I made it.

"I've got a lot to make up for," he said. "I am going to do it. I know I can. I never felt like this before and believe me I've taken the 'cures' which just dry you out for the next drunk.

"But send me a clipping of what you write, will you? Maybe some day I will need something to remind me about Hazelden again."

"I will, Vic," I said as we shook hands. "But promise me one thing. I will say that you have licked this thing. Don't make a liar out of me."

The Spire of St. Mary's

Time was when many of those in the neighborhood would look up as the sun caught the spire of St. Mary's Romanian Orthodox church at the corner of Atwater and Woodbridge and feel a twinge of longing.

For St. Mary's is a smaller, but exact duplicate of the church which stood in San-Nicolaul-Mare, Romania, whence came a large part of those who pioneered this little Romanian community in the city.

But the vanguard of people who first added the Romanian touch to the life of the city has dwindled with time.

Yet, while the sight of the dome rising to a point may not stir the second and third branches of the Romanian family trees to nostalgia for the homeland, the spirit and pride of their ancestors in Romanian traditions prevails.

And, with St. Mary's, its adjoining hall and new parish house as a focus, the Romanian neighborhood lies in the shadows, peopled by perhaps 60 families still, whose happiness and charming adherence to old world customs rises to the surface from time to time.

The Eastern European core is there in rollicking feet on the St. Mary's hall dance floor on a late Saturday night when they heed the music of the Hora.

And Baba Anna Lucki, "pastry queen" of the community, shawl over her head, sits and taps the time with her feet, and Mike (The Barber) Sarafolean watches, flanked by his sons, John, Nick and Steve, all barbers like him, and his daughter, Anna, a beautician.

Philip Toconita, for many years president of the parish, stands at the rear of the hall and says: "I am of the second generation—the link between the old and new.

"They came here sometime about the turn of the century to work in the packing houses and on the railroads. And their sons and sons' sons, in turn, shared the opportunity of America, the professions, business and education," he says.

Once there may have been 160 to 200 Romanian families living side by side in the neat, little houses, yards etched by picket fences. But some have moved with the city (and many passed away).

"Yet I think the core will always be here," says Phil.

If there were a single motto of these gracious, friendly people, it would be: Home, church and family.

To go to a Romanian wedding at St. Mary's is to see it all, unfolding.

Thus I went there on one crisp, November Saturday night at the hour of 7—when this Romanian wedding took place and watched pretty dark-haired Olivia Sonia married to Richard Hawkinson in a ritual of the Eastern Orthodox faith, solemn, yet colorful, and faintly suggestive of the Greek-oriental.

Long before that hour, the neighborhood filed into the church, in twos, threes and families. Out of the cold and into the warmth of the little church, where the fragrance of incense mingled with garlands of flowers.

In front the altar was hidden by a partition, broken by three gates. Only the priest can pass through the center gate. And at the right were the cantors.

The air of expectancy grew and at last the white carpet was unrolled and the principals began the wedding march to the front of the church, where Rev. Eugene Lazar of Gary, Indiana, waited. For him, a homecoming, since he was parish priest here for several years.

Olivia and Richard spoke their vows in a ceremony, read in English, instead of traditional Romanian, except at the very end. Bride and groom each accepted a white crown, symbolizing the crowning glory of marriage. Then each kissed the crown and took communion.

As they neared the back door, the spell was broken. Laughter and gaiety broke through the veneer. The couple left the church in a rain of coins, showered on them by relatives, and, ran around the corner to the hall, where already Gulesh and his orchestra, direct from Chicago, were striking up the fast rhythm of the Batuta.

"Nobody enters until he feeds the good luck well," he shouted.

The surging guests broke at the stairs, half going upstairs to swing to the tempo. The others converged on the basement. Here, in the steam of the kitchen, Mrs. Toconita wiped her brow. "One hundred chickens are frying," she says. And how many pounds of fried rice, Romanian style. At the urns, Sylvia David was brewing gallons of coffee. "We have been here, some all night and today," says Mrs. Toconita.

Famished, the guests fell to, and never-ending lines of waitresses kept filling the plates with more and more fried chicken until one could only hold up a wavering hand and cry: "No more !"

"Attention, folks!" Matt Duvlea was banging on a serving bowl. "We will now see what this marriage is worth to the relatives of the happy bride and groom." So saying, he and Phil Toconita passed the bowl to the bridal party. And the bowl soon was brimming—with checks and cash.

I was learning that generosity is a mark of a Romanian wedding, for which a Romanian bride can thank her luck to be so happily-born. For it is a poor wedding reception that nets only $2,000 and many run as high as $4,000 and $6,000.

Then, in a little half-serious, half-humorous ritual called the veiling, kindly hands of the other matrons lifted the veil off Olivia's head and tied a ribbon around it instead, all the while gathered around and chanting a melancholy Romanian song that spoke of the ages.

"Now," said John Folea at my elbow, "she has taken her place as a married woman in our community."

So the night wore on and the hall shivered with dancing feet; dozens of men paid as much as $5 each to dance with the red-cheeked bride.

And for just a brief interlude, Mr. Toconita took me across the courtyard to a big, modern new home—but strangely empty and dark.

"Our new parish house for a permanent priest we don't have," he said sadly. "There is a priest in Yugoslavia, but who knows when they will let him come to us? When we built this house, we had such high hopes. Into this place has gone the spirit as well as the money and muscle of our community."

He slapped me on the back, suddenly, and said:

"But come, we are talking about tomorrows. And forgetting the joys of tonight."

(There is a postscript. The priest from Yugoslavia has now arrived and "tomorrow" has become a happy "today" for the folks at St. Mary's.)

The Warehouse Wears a Halo

If you go along Lafayette road, north from E. Seventh deep in lower downtown St. Paul, the hulking warehouses and factories keep blotting out any mental image of the comfortable, big homes that once stood behind the trees which arched the quiet street.

It is difficult to think that where you walk so once walked men named Ireland, Hill and Prince, one to become an archbishop of unequaled stature in the city he helped build, another to be called the "Empire Builder" and the third a bank president.

And yet there is still a landmark of that time in the city. At the corner of Lafayette road and Ninth. An old limestone shell of what you immediately recognize as a church. Now a warehouse of the Lampland Lumber Co. Probably the most hallowed warehouse any lumber company ever occupied.

For this shell is that of old St. Mary's Catholic church, which for a half century shared—with the third Cathedral—the distinction of being the oldest Catholic churches standing in the city and, for one decade, old St. Mary's held that title alone.

As you stand about where the altar was located 90 years ago, lumber now stacked on either side in shelves, you are at the center of religious life for all of Catholic faith who lived in this once fashionable, pioneer core of old St. Paul—Lowertown.

Though the big towering spires are long gone and all but the shell obliterated, it still stands—old St. Mary's, and its present tenants, the Lamplands, regard it still with reverence and appreciation of the noble past.

This, for St. Mary's, began in 1865 with a proposal by Catholics in Lowertown that a church be built in their area, nearer than the Cathedral or Assumption Catholic church—the first Assumption, started in 1854 for German Catholics.

So a tract was purchased at what was then Ninth and Locust, one end fronting on quiet, shady Lafayette Park—of which the only remnant today is that triangle of ground in front of Sanitary Farm Dairies, Inc.

It is interesting to note that enthusiasm for the church was shared by Catholics and non-Catholics alike. And the roll call of first contributors includes such names, besides Hill and Prince, as governor H. H. Sibley and banker John L. Merriam; Thompson Bros., bankers; Henry M. Rice, the famed senator; Davidson, Donovan, Ullmann, Oakes, Amherst H. Wilder, Reardon, Borup, Dunn, Beaupre and Markoe.

The cornerstone was laid May 20, 1866, a day of celebration for the city in general. Led by the Great Western band, the religious marchers wound to the new church site, from the Cathedral, down Seventh and Eighth, on Broadway and Ninth, girls in white dresses, Bishop Thomas L. Grace in a carriage.

It is interesting about that cornerstone. You see, it has never been located to the knowledge of those with whom I have talked. So that, unless you probe the records, there is no date on the old building.

But the cornerstone is still there, probably buried under the ground in one of the footings which so far has not been uncovered.

Msgr. James M. Reardon, who ferreted out details of that occasion, reports that a hermetically sealed receptacle was placed inside the stone.

And those who, some day, open that "time capsule" will find issues of the old *Pioneer* (*Pioneer Press*), legal tender notes of that time, and a dedicatory parchment, the inscription written in Latin.

Thus, with pomp and on an auspicious note, did the pastor, Rev. Louis E. Caillet begin to shepherd his little flock, though the first mass was not held there until July 28, 1867.

The first sermon was preached by a priest named John Ireland, pastor of the Cathedral, due to become the great and much-loved archbishop. For him it was a homecoming since Lowertown was the bedrock of his family, the place where he grew up.

So St. Mary's grew and flourished and, as adjuncts, there were started and built a school, adjoining the church; the Convent of the Visitation at 318 Somerset, a home for girls at 571 Westminster, a day nursery and an institute for the deaf at 537 Mississippi.

Oh, those were golden, ambitious and rewarding years for old St. Mary's. And yet, in the background, was foreboding change. The city changed and the people went with it. One by one the old families moved away and railroads and smoke, dirt and noise, factories and warehouses crept nearer, began choking the life out of the parish.

There was yet one glorious moment for the old church—its Golden Jubilee on July 29, 1917—when Archbishop Ireland came back to preach the sermon as he had the first and not so long before his death.

Then, on a cold, February Sunday in 1922, the last mass was said there and the church closed—the parish reopened in its new and present building at Eighth and Rosabel.

There, if you go around to see the pastor, Rev. John Pilger, he will open the old baptism records and show you the penned names of the James J. Hill children. And in the church point out a beautiful, valued oil painting that once hung in old St. Mary's—a picture of Christ breaking the bread for His disciples, the painting given to the church by James J. Hill and now worth thousands of dollars.

Shorn as it may be of original stature, old St. Mary's can still be seen in White Bear Lake. Because the church of St. Mary's of the Lake there is an exact replica of the church at Lafayette and Ninth.

Where We Live

The West Side Is Really South

I don't imagine visitors and new arrivals in St. Paul are here long before they are leaning over the Kellogg Boulevard wall railing, waggling a finger and asking: "What part of town's that over there across the river?"

That, you say, is the "West Side." And behind it is West St. Paul and behind that South St. Paul.

"I beg your pardon," says the newcomer. "But I have a compass here that shows we have been looking south all the time. So you show me the West Side and West St. Paul and then South St. Paul. Remarkable."

So saying, he may turn on his heel and veer on line with magnetic north to the nearest coffee shop to ponder the quaint confusion.

Had it not been for a visit paid me some months ago by the late Ernest Stiefel, long regarded as a source of historic data about that section of the city across the river, I would not be able to clear up this directional dilemma.

Unreasonable as it may sound, that section in question is both west and south, but really it is not the West Side.

(You better get out that compass again.)

"It all began," said Mr. Stiefel, setting down a beautiful bouquet of peonies on my desk, "with the old steamboat pilots and captains who pioneered this region.

"Now, for a steamboat captain, there are only two directions—the west bank and the east bank—of a river.

"Well, sir, if you will consult your map, you will see that this area across the river, looking south, is actually the west bank of the Mississippi and where we are sitting is the east bank. And that's how the district in question got to be commonly known as the "West Side."

"But," added Mr. Stiefel, "we now come to the core of the discussion. Not everybody realizes that—officially—it is not correct to call the West Side the West Side.

"It has been, since 1917, known as 'Riverview,' a change that was voted by the citizens in that area."

And I got the impression that to call it the "West Side" is a little like calling San Francisco "Frisco" to a loyal citizen thereof.

The drama behind the story of how the name was changed to "Riverview" was related to me by Mr. Stiefel, who took a leading role on stage. In fact he was the "father of Riverview."

Confusion is what prompted it.

The West Side Commercial club was constantly getting confused with the West End Commercial club and West St. Paul.

"The board of directors, with one exception, wanted to change the name to the South Side Commercial club," he said.

Mr. Stiefel was that lone exception.

And on April 23, 1917, he held a mass meeting in the club hall. Four hundred turned out and it was generally conceded that nobody wanted to rename the West Side the South Side.

But no decision was reached that night and on Sept. 3 at a special membership meeting—only 35 attending—they sneaked "South Side" over on the others.

Mr. Stiefel didn't see "red" he saw the women. And it was they, organizing as the still flourishing Riverview Civic club, who got action. The sixth ward was divided into 12 districts.

A woman was chairman of each district. Housewives were marshalled and the Civic club canvassed the ward, leaving ballots at each home.

When the 3,561 votes were counted, 3,434 favored "Riverview," 50 balloted for "South Side," 35 for "West Side" and 15 for an assortment of names.

Except for a little kibitzing and heckling from the "east bank," the entire district swung behind "Riverview" with enthusiasm.

Encouraged by the will of the people, the committee pushed on to have the name used throughout the area. The telephone exchange was changed from Robie to Riverview; the West Side Postal station adopted Riverview as its official name and in April of 1918, the Commercial club changed its name from South Side to Riverview.

Of later years, lamented Mr. Stiefel, folks have been slipping back into their "West Side" ways. And it is his fervent hope—and certainly that of the ladies of the Riverview Civic club—that there should be a revival of "Riverview."

And that "West Side" be forever banished to the place where erroneous information goes.

Let me say that whoever travels across the river into the "West Bank" can do nothing but agree that no name ever fit a place more perfectly than "Riverview."

So all together now: "R-I-V-E-R-V-I-E-W."

Upper Levee Lore

If you stand on the High Bridge, a little way out from the north end and look down, you will see it below, some of the houses lying in the shadow of the big span— this tiny town within a city. They call it Upper Levee.

And each morning hundreds of cars pour off the Highland slopes and skirt the little village along Upper Levee road at the riverside. Yet I'll wager that though they pass by twice a day, not many motorists discover the town that lies behind the front row of buildings.

Only three blocks wide, to be sure, and not more than eight or nine blocks long—but packed with the happiness and sorrow, music and laughter of a community—mostly Italian families—that has watched Old Man River roll past its doorsteps a good three-quarters of a century.

For those of you who revel in the atmosphere of a down-river town, look not beyond Upper Levee. Here, lining either side of the narrow, 30-foot-wide streets—Loreto, Mill and Spring—are the kind of fences Tom Sawyer whitewashed.

Those towering cottonwoods at the river bank come with branches angled just right to support a barefoot youngster who likes to daydream as the towboats pass, or maybe drop a line in from a bamboo pole.

And the little plots of ground where the tomatoes grow big, red and ripe.

There, on a lot between Mill and Upper Levee road, the old schoolhouse once stood, the town hall for Upper Levee folk. And Miss Davenport, the kindergarten teacher, used to stand at the doorway and call the children in from recess. Under the watchful eye of the grand old lady of the neighborhood, Mrs. Mary Vanelli, who lived at 365 Mill.

And "Prof." Norton used to drive by at 7:30 p.m. and refuse to leave until the car was loaded with boys bound for the youth club meeting.

Sheriff Tommy Gibbons, it was, who came down to the school one night and said a thing that won him parental approval.

"I have never had any trouble with any of you boys and girls down here and do you know why?"

"No," chorused the little voices.

"Because," said Tommy, "your fathers know how to use their belts."

The school and "grandma" Vanelli have been gone a long time and the site is a vacant lot, dignified by the city as Mill playground, undoubtedly the smallest and most poorly equipped playground in the city. It has no equipment at all.

The upper levee is a community where nearly everybody was or is related to everybody else. And the names read like Vanelli, Sauro, Fritz (for Fratangelo), De Maio, Crea and De Carlo. And Frank Marzitelli, the commissioner of public works, grew up there and his homestead is still standing as sturdy as ever.

The village was a place of tradition—dancing, round-robin style in homes every Saturday night years ago; the "Carnivalle" before Lent, when, as they do in Italy, folks wore masks and costumes and roamed the streets.

And the men rolled a game of "pellans" down the narrow streets on Sundays. And twice a year followers of St. Anthony or St. Joseph went to the river bank, built big fires and sang holy songs on the Saints' days while the youngsters roasted potatoes in the hot coals. The community was pretty evenly divided—St. Anthony group and the St. Joseph contingent.

Pigeon racing still is popular on the Levee, and you can talk to such enthusiasts as Mike, Nick, and Chris Sauro—related but not brothers—and Louie De Maio or Frank De Carlo. Sometimes they'll drive 500 miles to release a pigeon.

"But the old days are disappearing; now it is not so much like it was in the past," said Mrs. Rose Fritz.

"Those were days," I was told, "when Vanelli's grocery store was on Mill street and Charley Jannetto's tavern was a focus for the old men and one day we sat and watched a man jump to his death from the High bridge. We could only watch, in horror."

"So now, I hear, they are going to take away the Levee and industrialize it," she says. "It is too bad, but that's progress, I guess.

"A man builds a house with his hands and lives in it all his life and then along comes progress."

Autumn in Frogtown

There is a time to make a pilgrimage into that little pocket of the city called "Frogtown." I would pick an afternoon in late fall when the blue dusk is settling across the neat, fenced-in yards and the hour of 5 p.m. chimes from the clock in the baroque steeple of old St. Agnes.

It is this time of the day and the year when the spell of timelessness hangs over this section of the city, bounded roughly by University and Minnehaha, Western and Dale.

When the last of the storm windows are going on over kitchen panes, brightly-lighted, and the room filtering into the sharp evening the aromas of baking bread, broiling sausages and sauerkraut, pot roast or roasting turkey in the fullest Germanic traditions.

For it is a thing of pride that though the city marched beyond its boundaries and left it one of the oldest parts of St. Paul, Frogtown has escaped the "rounded-at-the-heels" look. Through generation after generation, Frogtowners have stayed to enjoy the fruits of a "Gemütlichkeit" found among friendly neighbors. The old folks have given way to sons and daughters who, in turn have gone into the suburbs to look and then come back to the neighborhood of their birth to stay. And many one-family houses have been turned into multiple dwellings.

Thus the number of children scaling the picket and wire fences and swinging on the gates, is as large as 50 years ago.

In the lore of "Frogtown," a number of legends have grown during the three-quarters of a century, which has blended frugal, well-scrubbed citizens and melded an appreciation of good beer, food, deep religious conviction and a love of sports and the rhythm of a polka.

Not the least legend is the origin: "Frogtown."

The one most generally accepted story is that "Frogtown" stems from the fact that once the district was covered by a marsh, one of whose characteristics was a preponderance of frogs in good and loud voice.

The other story of "Frogtown" is that the name refers—in impolite slang—to the fact that a number of French settled the area in its early history. There is basis in fact for this, too.

A gentleman named Benjamin Lafond, for instance, was instrumental in naming some of the principal thoroughfares of Frogtown—Lafond, after himself, Edmund, Charles, and Thomas, after relatives, and Blair after a young lady friend.

As you walk the streets on this waning autumn day with a "Frogtown" native, you pause at one of the commercial corners—Kent and Edmund. Except for fresh paint and stucco here and there, it stands unchanged.

The little tavern on one corner which once was Henry Jurgensen's meat market, where the quarters of beef and whole hogs hung in the cooler and Saturday in the shop was spicy with fresh sausage.

And you cross the street to Adam's furniture store and funeral home—a combination typical of small communities. And around the corner, in his living room, Roman Adam relaxes and goes back into the history of "Frogtown" as he knows it and his father, George, knew it.

That side of the intersection has been "Adam's corner" since 1886. Before that—beginning in 1868—the building was two saloons. One entrance led into Yoerg's tavern, the other into Schmidt's.

Sitting alongside the big window, looking back on the old Adam stable, you hear Roman Adam go back, too, to names in his ken:

George Ries, of Milton and Thomas, once county auditor who used to translate German in city hall; John Asfalg, the grocer on Thomas; the Hermes block at Thomas and Dale; Tschida's hall at Lafond and Arundel and old Plebuch hall, once the center for dances.

Dietsch's hall, Thomas and Western, is the only one left.

You leave Adam's and walk past the places he has mentioned and the houses, some set close to the sidewalks.

So you come to an institution in Frogtown—the "Nickel Joint"—at 501 Blair, a place whose name brings back ancient days of nickel beer and free lunches, not only an oasis, but headquarters for the Frogtown athletic club and the Oldtimer's Hot Stove league, whose members decorated the back hall with 166 photographs—a priceless "Cooperstown Hall of Fame" of St. Paul baseball history since 1877.

North End "Monuments" Still Offer Vivid Memories

I went out Rice Street the other day and refreshed some memories, met some ghosts and discovered landmarks I should have seen long ago.

They call it the North End now. For me, it's that piece of the quilt from University to Larpenteur, from Jackson Street to Western. But Rice is the main blacktop artery of many hues, with its veins of streets and houses hunched together as they always have been. And there are the domes and spires of the Polish patch around St. Adalbert's and the Romanian slice at Woodbridge and Atwater, where the spire of St. Mary's Romanian Orthodox Church stands.

I wonder if they still have weddings there on Saturday nights like the one I once attended 30 years ago, with its pageantry and dancing and feasting into the dawn?

I drove up Rice, and just north of Como, I remembered the Pioneer Sausage shop was there and went inside to buy some of the "Weiss Wurst"—veal bratwurst. I looked in vain for Joe Knoedjen, who started it all back in the years before World War II. Those afternoons in the 1950s we'd chat in the back room, where the smokers were curing the bacons, hams, sausages and we'd sample some and Joe would hand around big mugs of beer.

I drove on, passing a building where there once was a dance hall and meeting room on the second floor. It was there I interviewed Oscar Johnson one night and he told me how he and Eddie Shipstad and the old Shop Pond Gang near the Great Northern yards spawned skaters who became the world-famous Ice Follies.

I moseyed through the district around Faith Lutheran church and recalled all the times I'd spent gathering the stories the Rev. Charles L. Grant used to tell there in the church he founded in 1914. He always had a tabulation ready about the thousands of baptisms, marriages, funerals and confirmations he'd performed. And one night I emceed and spoke at Pastor Grant's and his wife's golden wedding anniversary. Now, they're both in Wilder Infirmary. He'll be 96 in January.

I went up Rice Street, passing a storefront, where a street social worker once spent his time, combing the vacant lots, back alleys, culverts, bars and all-night cafes for young people in trouble, runaways. I spent an afternoon with him and met a few of his failures. The successes, he told me, are long gone.

Rice Street had a reputation for being the "toughest street in town" and young men from "outside" took their lives in their hands if they became enamored of Rice Street girls. Or so the folklore ran. But maybe the fault was that it had a bad press.

Somewhere on my route I remembered Weyandt's furniture store and saw Muntean's Sport Shop, but when I wrote about it in the 1960s it was Muntean-Heddman and one of the most fashionable general stores in the city.

And how many times I've browsed Caron Fabre's world of antique-styled furniture and lampshades. There it was, curious as ever.

The dark hulk of old Washington High School stood silhouetted against the mist of the afternoon. The last time I was at an assembly there, the students were honoring a local boy who made good, LeRoy Neiman, the Rice Street dropout who became one of the western world's most accomplished and visible artists. Tschida's Bakery is still there, but not under the management I knew 30 years ago, when you'd try to get there at the right time on the right day for its fabulous German rye. The present owners have kept the faith.

The distinctive twin octagonal spires of St. Bernard's Catholic Church reach into the rainy sky as they have since 1905. They are striking pieces of architecture.

In that Austrian-German citadel of Catholic community, St. Bernard's spires are a reassuring symbol of that Rice Street steadiness of lifestyles, devotion to traditions of hard work, family and unwavering faith. I parked the car and walked up closer to admire them.

I watched the children going home from the school. As I saw some of their mothers and teachers I wondered whether they appreciate their church as much as I did?

The children reminded me of the Rev. Romauld K. Bloms, the "Iron Hand in the Velvet Glove" who, as St. Bernard's high school principal in the late 1960s, ran a tight ship that became a model of education. He was admired, respected and envied by other educators—and some students—in that age of unsettled growing up.

His school was part of the core of culture that St. Bernard's spread through the community, with such groups as the Drama Club, founded in 1916. It was a prolific producer of live theater, which filled the gaps between radio, movie houses and television.

There was a tiny Swiss colony there, too, in the hollow between Maryland and Larpenteur, where I once gathered an afternoon's worth of Swiss lore from the few families still in residence. High rises, condos fill those spaces now.

I found my way back toward the Loop, via St. Vincent's Parish along Virginia Street, on the edge of Rice Street territory. This was the Irish "homeland" of the late businessman Joseph L. Shiely Sr., who never tired of telling me that the parish really should have been called St. Patrick's but some "East Siders got the jump on us" and "they'd never even seen a leprechaun."

Farewell to Swede Hollow

It was late on a crisp November afternoon when I stood astride a trickling creek and looked up a long ravine, at the desolation and wreckage of a crevice in the city that has, for a better part of 116 years, been known as Swede Hollow.

And as I looked at the sagging, empty shells of shacks and houses, remnants of one of the weirdest neighborhoods ever nestled in a city, I could hear far above, on either side, the traffic noises of St. Paul's lower East Side.

It was odd, I thought, that though bounded by Payne Avenue and E. Seventh Street, none who drove along those thoroughfares was perhaps aware of the little world—older than the city—that existed there for more than a century.

But the city has issued the eviction notices—declaring the place unfit for human habitation—and has hopes that in the not too distant future Swede Hollow will be filled in (it will be a mighty task) and industrialized with something bright and new and shiny.

Swede Hollow has been an enigma, shabby and a little on its uppers, ever since Edward Phelan (Phalen or Faylen) built his crude cabin at the head of the ravine, where Hamm's brewery now stands, in 1839. And except for brief bursts of unorganized housecleaning, Swede Hollow went along its disorganized way to the moment I stood there—in 1956—straddling what once was a lusty, rushing flow of water called Phalen creek and for whom the ravine's single, lackadaisical street was named.

For Swede Hollow, life has been a series of cycles of nationalities—beginning with the Swedes who settled there first and called the place "Svenska Dalen," from which was derived Swede Hollow. And then came the Irish and later the Italians and finally the Mexicans.

And scattered through the city you will find many a family whose ancestry dates back to the carefree, informal ways of the Hollow where the youngsters dangled their feet in the creek water and the scene always came with the same old props, the yellow cur, the quacking duck and long-necked goose.

City ordinances against taming wildlife or housing domestic fowl, goats and lambs never bothered the Hollow folk in the least. They just built their little board passes over the creek, hung their out-houses over the water, dug wells, erected fences and followed natural whims and eccentricities of householding.

For the hollow are no proud memories such as those of a Summit Avenue or a Williams Hill or Irvine Park. Only the constant shabbiness, unkempt life—and intrigue.

Even in the beginning there appeared a blot on its good name.

Founder Phalen has, through history's pages, been branded as the murderer of his cabinmate in that long ago—an ex-sergeant Hays, whose battered body was found back in 1839 in the water near Carver's cave.

What street or neighborhood could live down such an incident in the launching of its career?

These things crossed my mind as I roamed the ghost town in the Hollow, where faded worn teddy bears had been left sprawling in the yards, along with football helmets, tin cans, bottles and old portable bathtubs.

But here, hold on a minute! Did I see, in the rubble, touches of pride? The neat stone walls, the picturesque grape arbors, the careful landscaping?

Maybe I have been wrong in my assessment. Perhaps there was, in Swede Hollow, like any other neighborhood, a twinge of melancholia when the last farewells were said, when the shrill echoes of children's laughter spanning a century no longer peal off the cliff sides.

Like the Sea of Galilee

The shadows from the mighty trees lining the parking lot were just beginning to blend into darkness when the cars began pulling into the lot alongside Como Park pavilion.

Out beyond, in the traffic circle, the lights played their colors across the spray of the fountain, lighting momentarily the Sunday evening strollers moving slowly toward the pavilion lights, strung around the cornices.

They came singly and in couples, some holding hands; there were families and groups of teen-agers and a busload from the Union Gospel Mission. There were picnickers, pausing on the way home after a day in the park.

Sports clothes, sports coats, ties and flowery shirts.

In the sky, lightning flashed. Beyond the pavilion patio, through the pillars, the lights sparkled off the still lake waters. Moving on the further shore the pairs of headlights of cars.

Up on the pavilion stage, the Souls Harbor TV choir was moving onto the risers. A pretty girl, Barbara Wentworth, in white with a flower in her hair, played a rambling sort of hymn on the organ.

Then, at 9:30 p.m., the music stopped. A gentleman in a dark suit coughed experimentally into the microphone and then he began.

"Welcome, welcome, folks. To the annual season of Twin City Community Hymn Sings. We're going to meet every other Sunday again this year. It's nice to see so many back again, even though the weather has been threatening.

"But it's a wonderful night and here we are ending the Sabbath together. So let's all sing with everything we've got. Sing our praises to the Lord."

Thus did Hugo W. Hagstrom, St. Paul businessman, begin the season for one of the most unusual community traditions in any city. One which he originated because he thought it was a nice way for a city to end Sunday.

And for the next hour, at the direction of Dr. Orville Aftreth of Robbinsdale, that crowd sang the old hymns with thundering, ringing voices that carried far across the waters of the lake.

With Tom Anderson on the trumpet and recording artist Eddy Menaldeno, harpist Marjorie Lagerwall and violinist Richard Salini to urge them on. And the choir.

The way the crowd sang "Battle Hymn of the Republic" would have done credit to a professional massed choir of 2,000 voices.

They opened with that and then Dr. Aftreth began reading the words of the next song "When the trumpet of the Lord shall sound, and time shall be no more . . ."

And the audience pealed out the wonderful words and melody of "When the Roll Is Called Up Yonder, I'll Be There."

"Doesn't it do something to you? Doesn't it send chills up and down your spine?" cried Dr. Aftreth when the last note had faded into the night wind that sent gusts of dust and loose hymn booklets skittering through the pavilion.

And it did do something to you, all right.

"Ah, is everyone happy here tonight?" shouted Dr. Aftreth. "If you are, smile at your neighbor."

The audience got a little rest while the guests on stage sang and played, Mr. Menaldeno singing one of his recording favorites, "Nearing the Shore."

And if you listened carefully, you could hear the children and some of their parents, a young couple sitting near the back, humming the tunes.

You noticed, too, that although there was nothing said, out of respect for the occasion, not one person smoked during the entire hour.

Finally, Dr. Aftreth moved back to the microphone, after Mayor Dillon had welcomed them to the city, and the audience tuned up again on "Shall We Gather at the River."

Though the rain and wind of a storm broke around them outside, few left before they had sung "Now the Day is Over" and "God Be With You Until We Meet Again."

Then it was over and the crowd filed past the boys holding cardboard boxes and dropped coins in the "collection" plates.

But I thought most of them left a little reluctantly. There were still a lot more songs they could have sung—and I could have listened to.

And as I watched them and heard them singing, looking over 2,000 faces, on a Sunday night, I got a warm feeling about the people of a city who will turn out to sing the Old Hymns at the lakeside as neighbors, yet having met only a few minutes earlier.

It takes a lot more than buildings and streets and odd nooks and crannies and concrete and steel to create a good city. It takes something like 2,000 people sitting in Como Park pavilion on Sunday night, singing in reverence and enthusiasm.

Buying and Selling

House of Real Make Believe

A knight's coat of armor stands guard just inside the door and a clown's mask leers from the wall. There is a faint blend of mothballs and wool. And when you close the door, you seal out the world of Wabasha and Sixth Streets.

It is silent in the high-ceilinged rooms, except for the whirring of a fan and Rose Joos' sewing machine somewhere offstage. And yet the echoing laughter and tears of a hundred operas, a thousand plays, thousands more masked balls and parties, operettas and carnivals pour off the racks bulging with clothing, from the boxes stacked on the floor and on shelves.

For you are standing in the House that Martin Giesen built, on the second floor of the Midland building, in the heart of a city which is scarcely aware that the Northwest's oldest theatrical costume shop is here.

Giesen's is the wonderful magic place where—since 1872—a man or woman, girl or boy has been turned into anything and anybody he or she has always wanted to be: Napoleon, Queen Elizabeth, Cinderella, Prince Charming, Hitler, Marie Antoinette, a lion, tiger, camel and horse, Santa Claus or the devil, King Arthur or Teddy Roosevelt, General U. S. Grant, Abe Lincoln or George Washington, Caesar and Cleopatra, the Big Bad Wolf and Little Red Ridinghood.

141

All these and thousands upon thousands more characters—fact and fiction—down through the centuries have come from the House of Giesen.

The Fairy Godmother who makes this transformation is a charming woman, who gets up from behind her desk to shake hands—Mrs. Olga Giesen. And until he died in 1943, her husband, Martin, was the Fairy Godfather. By merely taking a costume off a rack, lifting a wig out of a box, a suit off a hanger, a mask off a shelf—they performed these miracles.

For them all the world was truly a stage and all the actors merely players. Except, for Olga and Martin it became a real place of make believe.

With uncanny memory, nearly everyone at Giesen's can locate—within a minute—the false whiskers, pages' costumes, togas and sandals, bows and arrows, hassocks and cassocks, crowns of jewels and thorns.

And tell the stories that go with each.

Of midnights in the Christmas holiday seasons of yore when the rooms were crowded with celebrants, standing in line to return and rent costumes in a carnival spirit shared by all but the weary Giesens.

Or the day F. Scott Fitzgerald and a friend rented costumes for the famous author's first play, and of a fabulous holiday night when F. Scott and a taxi-driver descended upon a fashionable Summit Avenue party, inside a Giesen camel.

"Scott wrote a story about that party. It opened in our shop," said Olga.

There were the exciting days when Maude Adams, Chauncey Alcott and Ethel Barrymore came in person or via wardrobe managers to have costumes made.

"But come," said Olga, "let us tour. And I will tell you a few stories about our place . . . and you can try on one of the few hand-made Civil War uniforms left in the world . . . or duck your head into this beautiful lion's head."

In the second room she paused in front of a rack of military uniforms. "This one," she said, "is almost a shrine. It is the U. S. Air Corps uniform that belonged to Dick Flemming, medal of honor winner who died crash-bombing his plane against the Japs."

She picked up a Civil War hat. "We had another hat like it once," she said. "Bought it in a hock shop in New York City. A few years later there was a big parade of Civil War veterans in St. Paul. And an old man came in to rent a Civil War cap. He picked up this particular hat and suddenly spied the faded Army serial number on the inside. Tears rolled down his cheeks. 'This was my buddy's cap in the war,' he said. 'He died a long time ago.'" Mrs. Giesen made him a present of the hat.

"Over on this rack," she said, "is a Canadian air force uniform from World War I. It belonged to Richard Arlen, the movie actor. Dick came in one day to visit—long before he was a star. So happened that another lad was in the shop trying to rent a Canadian air force uniform. We didn't have any, so Dick said we could use his. The lad who rented it never returned the uniform and I paid Dick for it. Then, one day long after, an old man came in. He said his son had been arrested and he had found the uniform, which he wanted to return. I asked him why his son had been jailed.

"'For impersonating a Canadian air force officer in this uniform,' the father said sadly."

These are only fragments of the human drama locked in the boxes and folds of the House of Giesen.

She has earned the title of the Northwest "Emily Post" of theatrical costuming; her library is full of volumes on stagecraft.

"The hours are long, the telephone an incessant jangle, and sometimes I get so tired," she said. But the glamor and romance are overpowering. Where else, for instance, can you pause late at night, under the tiny lamp in the office, look across the room and see—in your mind—a procession of the world's personalities marching silently out of the shadows?

Romance on Market Row

Things aren't the way they used to be on City Market "row," they told me back in 1958.

I didn't argue. You don't argue with Simon Goldish and O. E. (Jack) Nelson. Simon is 82½ and Jack is 81 and they are the only ones left on market row along Jackson street who remember it all—64 years on the market.

"All right," I said, "things aren't the way they used to be—but how were they?" Simon looked at Jack. Jack looked out of the window of Simon's little office. My gaze followed his—across to the market row sheds, lined with parked cars, at the flower sellers.

His eyes paused a moment inside Simon's shed, surveying the crates of big, red tomatoes, baskets of onions, lettuce, oranges, sacks of potatoes. He sniffed the delicious and yet faintly earthy aroma of fresh vegetables and fruit. Like spring.

It was a tennis match, when they began to tell me. The two trading story for story, bouncing off my ears.

Simon told how it was when the market was on Third Street and you were late if you began romancing 180-pound sacks of potatoes around at 2 a.m. And a half century ago Bill Cooney used to signal the day's start by letting out a war whoop that woke all the guests in the nearby Merchants hotel, so that they had to silence him.

While Simon was gathering his breath, Jack chimed in, naming names that have threaded through market history—Jack Reilly, and the peddlers, Dobson and Lipschultz and poor Max Pheiffer who jumped to his death one morning from a room in the Hotel St. Paul.

And the La Nasas and "California" Joe Insera.

The grapefruit was unknown and Schoch's grocery finally agreed to take a few, which they displayed around the upstairs railing in the store. And a lady from Summit Avenue called and asked how you cook them. They had a phrase then: "If corn grew on Seventh street, would Schoch shock it?"

Those were the days—in the early 1900s—when the finest onions in the Northwest grew in the fields near Afton, Minnesota, on the St. Croix, and in the winter the entire city ate only two crates of tomatoes because they were a summertime food.

And five barrels of head lettuce from New Orleans took care of the city's needs for a week.

"It seems like only yesterday—but it really was 1897—when I sold 27 carloads of Concord grapes in one day," said Simon. "You could sell a carload of spinach off the sidewalk within a matter of hours and now you can't give it away."

"You'd work all day, six days a week and come down on Sundays," said Jack. "And you could stand on the street, on top of cases of fresh strawberries and sell them so fast it made your head swim. And keep an eye out for somebody stealing them from the edge of the pile."

Simon remembered the first time he saw a Washington apple and a navel orange. They were exotic fruits in St. Paul—reserved for the best tables in the best homes, hotels and clubs.

Ramsey county was a cucumber center, with as many as 12 carloads a day going out to Chicago, Boston and Philadelphia.

There were those summer mornings when the flood of fresh green groceries glutted the sheds in the new Jackson row and grocers loaded up like gluttons after the long winter's famine.

Long before dawn the sheds were sold out and the truck gardeners climbed back on their wagons and went back to harvest more.

You piled and haggled, cussed and perspired on steaming August mornings and froze and got chilblains loading and unloading freight cars of oranges and lemons in winter's blizzards. The icy winds blew snow into your shed and the coal stove in the little office never quite kept up with the cold.

"One morning I loaded 450 cases of strawberries between 2 and 5:30 a.m.," said Simon. "But those were days when you hired a wagon, team and driver for $110 a month—any time of the day or night he was on call."

"Do you remember the apple parades in 1920?" said Jack, pointing to a picture on the wall. It showed wagons loaded with apples, carrying homemade signs: "Solomon said: 'Comfort me with apples,'" "Oh, you pippin," and "Eat apples 24 hours a day."

Then something happened. Suburbia snuffed out the little truck gardens and sons no longer wanted to work small plots for a pittance when jobs in the city paid so much more. So the huge truck garden emerged as a full-grown business; somebody invented frozen foods; no longer did the city rely on what grew around it.

And, one by one the old-timers dropped back in the frantic pace to keep up with ever increasing carloads of fruits and vegetables that poured in—12 months a year—from around the world.

So now only Simon and Jack are left from the old guard that once made up the "most cosmopolitan row" in the city.

"I think I hated it all the time," said Simon. "These 64 years. Who would work like a slave in a business like this?"

"I loved it," said Jack. "Like you did. Or you wouldn't be here." They were arguing about whether they loved it or hated it when I left. But I had my answer. I knew how things used to be on the City market.

And how they're not like that anymore.

Kessel's Bakery

All day Saturday and again Sunday they came to the store at 244 E. Fairfield and sniffed deliciously at the aromas of baking and joshed with each other. And met old friends and gathered up their packages and left in order to make room for others.

Sometimes the crowds at Kessel's bakery spilled out onto the sidewalk that runs along the street with its old buildings flush with the concrete.

This was the weekend for the celebration of the Jewish New Year's and in St. Paul for the faithful that means at least one trip to Kessel's bakery. There are several reasons.

In the tradition that once was the Jewish community's on the West Side flats, Kessel's remains in the old neighborhood as a reminder of how it used to be. Like Mintz's shoe store, a few doors away.

And in time of celebration, or just on Sundays, you come down to the flats again to renew old acquaintances and recapture some of the warmth of the past. And this you do at Kessel's.

Besides, Kessel's is the only bakery in the Twin Cities that makes the bagels—Bernie Kessel calls them "Simonized doughnuts," in the old-country way, and also the special bread for the New Year called "fagel" which means "as a bird flies."

For the non-Jewish neighborhoods of the city, Kessel's is the institution of the famous pumpernickel sourdough roll and bread. Though I doubt that except for those who like atmosphere with their buying, few persons have even known where they might find Kessel's; the rolls and bread go to them—in stores and the best clubs in the city.

These are carried around the city by Joe Kessel, who is referred to as "the outside" member of the firm. In other words, he drives the truck. Bernie stays in the shop and bakes.

Joe used to be a mail truck driver, assigned to special delivery. That's when I met him. He would come into the *Dispatch* newsroom at night, deliver his mail, then use the managing editor's phone to check on some orders for rolls or bread.

He always carried a few baked goods orders along with his special delivery. But if anybody ever got rolls instead of a letter by mistake, they never mentioned it. More than likely Joe got a new customer. A special delivery letter and a Kessel pumpernickel roll were an unbeatable combination.

Oscar Kessel, who is responsible for all this, would raise his eyebrows off his head if he could see what has happened at 244 E. Fairfield.

Oscar came to America from Russia back about the turn of the century and brought with him his recipes for bagels and fagel and sourdough pumpernickel and about all the boys have done is make sure they followed papa's directions.

But on a much grander scale, using, for example, a 40-pan roll oven, the largest in the country, modern to the nth degree— except that they still use the old-country custom, dating back to the time of Moses, of baking on cornmeal, accounting for the crusty bottom—but never even singed beyond what it should be.

Maybe Oscar would not be so surprised at that. Kessel's personality hasn't changed since he left this earth. Mama Kessel— Zessel Kessel—still waits on the customers and commiserates about this and that. Hyman Chargo still comes in every day to ponder world affairs. Grandpa Frank's beard has turned white, but he still walks a few miles twice a week to buy his quota of baked goods. Mrs. Diamond comes in from a few houses away, like she has for 42 years. And she still says the same nice things about what a wonderful man, "God rest his soul," Oscar was.

Ben Mintz, who is Bernie's brother-in-law, runs over to help wait on the trade some days and if business is too fast—like it was over the weekend—Bernie has an emergency crew of men from the neighborhood who come over without being asked.

They just walk in and if it's busy, they go to work.

Or they chat. Because Kessel's is a wonderful place to trade gossip and births and deaths and engagements and retell old West Side lore—in between bagels and fagel.

They Never Leave Payne Avenue

Go up into that east side town within a city, Payne Avenue, any afternoon and buttonhole the first native you meet with this question:

"Why, sir, is it that the Scandinavians on the East Side are loath to ever move out of the area?"

And it's 10 to 1 the answer will be:

"Well, I don't know, except that they probably don't want to get too far away from the cinnamon toast at Jacobsen's bakery."

After hearing the same reply from the next half dozen persons, there is only one thing left:

Visit Jacobsen's bakery.

Here you have a choice, either Jacobsen's at 981 or 1097 Payne. The former if you wish to discover what it is that has created this Payne Avenue, nay East Side institution, whose cinnamon toast has been carried worldwide and guarded as carefully in transit as if it were gold.

Because it is at 981 that you will meet Miss Sigrid Jacobsen, daughter of the founder and first kneader of dough, Engvald Jacobsen, as staunch a Norwegian as ever invaded the domain of the Swede with a peace offering of Danish pastry.

And if it is on a late Friday afternoon, you will be caught up in a confusion of wedding cakes, racks full of doughnuts, coffee cakes, and always the cinnamon toast.

But Miss Jacobsen and the others in the back room are never too busy but what they won't bring out the big, white coffee pot and ask a stranger to dunk a piece of toast with them for hospitality's sake.

And I have it from others that the appetite of many a Payne Avenue citizen has been ruined because he wandered—lost among the pastries—into the back room by mistake just as the coffee cups were being filled.

In order to understand the lure of the cinnamon toast, you must comprehend that eating and dunking it in coffee is an old Scandinavian custom and once learned cannot be easily discarded.

Little Miss Jacobsen and her associates, modest as they may be, admit that their experience in toast making, dating back to 1907, has given them a lot of practice.

"I just can't say what it could be about the toast," says Miss Jacobsen. "It is only toast with sugar and cinnamon on it. Of course we do make it from roll dough and not bread."

And of course, the recipe for the dough is a family secret, although they all say: "But it is so simple."

And the finishing of the toast—that also is a family secret, not to mention that Harold Jacobsen, Miss Jacobsen's brother, is the only one who can blend the ingredients properly.

The toast goes to Chicago, California and across the ocean, carried in the hands of Jacobsen bakery pilgrims and not shipped.

"It isn't good for mailing," says Miss Jacobsen. "Although we do send some to East Side boys in service."

To give you an idea of how devoted to the toast East Siders are, one lad in uniform wrote home a few years ago and said all he wanted for Christmas was Jacobsen's cinnamon toast.

And Dr. Henry A. Holmberg, just around the corner, is reported to have said on the street the other day that apartment hunters of Swedish descent have been looking for vacancies in the proximity of the bakery.

To all of which, Miss Jacobsen and the Misses Marie Johnson and Amelia Anderson ("don't mind what last names you give us; just so there's a 'son' on the end") will laugh and say it isn't really so.

"And now, how about one more cup of coffee for the road?"

With cinnamon toast, of course.

Legend of Halls' Barber Shop

Walt Hadlich, fresh from San Francisco, came back to his home town of St. Paul the other day. And he hadn't been here long before he hustled over to Hall Bros. barber shop at 892 Selby, carrying his 7½-month-old grandson, Gerret B. Lok, III.

"Brought him all the way from California to get his first haircut," said Walt. "Got to make it four generations of Hadlichs who've had their hair cut in your shop."

And that sounded reasonable to Ed Hall. Seems as if in the late years old customers have been dropping in from all over the world, bringing the latest branches of the family tree to be properly trimmed at Ed's place.

This is the result of several accomplishments by the Hall boys. One undoubtedly is the skill with which they built a clientele of faithful followers over the past 60 years; another is the splendid location on Fifth near Wabasha that the Halls enjoyed for 47 years until they left the Loop in 1945 for the present abode (taking most of their pilgrims along).

But most important, perhaps, is Ed Hall, whose wit has been as sharp as the edge of his shaving razor and who has been variously labeled "That sly old fox," humanitarian and champion of his people—the Negroes of St. Paul.

Thus it is that Ed (S.E. he sometimes is called), his brother, O.C. (no longer in the shop) and Art, still on the shearing line, have clipped the famous heads of city and state.

Following them through, as it were, from the time they were curly-headed cherubs to the billiard-balled finish.

"'Bout every customer I got now," Ed said the other day, "is somebody I got from another generation."

Ed has had a faculty for consorting, tonsorially speaking, with the "big names."

Before he opened his own shop, Ed worked in Howard's barber parlor in the old Gilfillan block next to the Merchants hotel, at Fourth and Jackson.

"One day," says Ed, "Frank Day, the Fairmont publisher, walked into the shop and said, 'Boys, I want you to meet the next governor of Minnesota.

"I looked up at the tall, gangling fellow," says Ed. "And I didn't say much, being a Republican all my life. But Mr. Day was right. That fellow was the next governor—John A. Johnson."

When he was snipping away in his once-famous locale at 12 E. Fifth Street, Ed entertained Governors Van Sant and Floyd B. Olson from time to time. Shaves, mostly.

In 1906, when Ed left Howard's and moved up on Fifth, he took with him about 14 or 15 shaving mugs, tangible evidence that he had at least that many customers.

Inscribed on the mugs were such names as J. M. Burbank, now retired vice president of Farwell, Ozmun, Kirk & Co., who has been a steady patron of Ed's from the beginning and F. I. Whitney, once general passenger agent of the Great Northern railway.

The intimate era of the personal shaving mug passed, but not the association between Ed and the men whose chin whiskers and mustaches he trimmed and shaved.

It was Mr. Whitney who, upon hearing Ed had been married, said: "Go ahead and take my nine-room house at Chatsworth and Iglehart. It's more than we need. Pay me for it when you can."

Ed moved in, complete with one bedroom suite which was all the furniture he owned. And he lives at the same address today.

When Shreve Archer died a few years ago, Ed knew him so well he erected a memorial in his honor at Pilgrim Baptist church, where Ed is the oldest trustee.

In all the city there never was a place like Halls' barber shop on Fifth, with its assortment of gay bottles filled with colored liquids, and the aroma of bay rum and shaving soap to tantalize the nostrils.

And the atmosphere filled with repartee, as pungent as the sting of the after shave lotions. Almost legend are the incidents that were hatched at Halls'.

Like the morning that Dr. Jim Quinn drove up with horse and buggy, looping the reins around the barber pole at the curbside. When he left the shop, Dr. Quinn went over to Parker's drug store across the street, forgetting his horse. But the horse didn't forget him and strolled along behind, ripping the barber pole out of its socket and carrying it nonchalantly dangling from the reins.

And the day Police Chief John O'Connor, almost a fixture at Halls', came in and dropped four or five ducks on the floor and said to his right bower, a man named Nugent: "Take these over to the mayor (Larry Ho)." Just then His Honor walked in and Chief O'Connor told him: "Larry, I'm sending some ducks over to you; now you just hang them out the window so they'll stay cold."

When the mayor had gone, the chief called a man named Davis in the fire department, located on the basement level of the city hall, and said:

"Listen, if you've got a long pole, I know where you can get some ducks that are hanging out of a second-story window. Now, I know where they came from and it's all right. They're yours. Just get that pole and bring 'em down."

So Davis did and the mayor never did find out what happened to his ducks.

There was a young fellow, bookkeeper, who kept running over from across the street to get a haircut and since so many doctors were in the same building, Ed thought this young man was a physician and kept calling him "doc." And still does, although the "doc" really is Herbert Buetow, president of Minnesota Mining & Manufacturing.

Ed recalls the time Chief O'Connor's man, Nugent, who had a weakness for candy, kept dipping into the chief's pocket and found the tastiest, chocolate-covered morsels.

"Unfortunately," said Ed, "the candy that day had unusual medicinal qualities, which Nugent soon discovered."

So it went at Halls' barber shop where Democrats fought Republicans orally all day long, but where it was a rule that every barber had to cut with a bi-partisan attitude in mind.

Passing of the Pool Parlor

I guess there weren't too many around the day when Bilbow's billiard parlor closed up there at 443 St. Peter.

In the press of the hurry, hurry up and down St. Peter and the myriad problems a city gets itself involved in, there were only a few for whom the name Bilbow's still kindled a flame of an era.

When it closed, Bilbow's wasn't even in the proper setting for those who might remember the 40 or so years when Bilbow's was synonymous with billiards and pool in St. Paul.

Then it was located down on Minnesota, near the Bremer Arcade. Those were the days when billiard-playing was the fashion and the young bucks sighted down a cue like their sons swing a golf club or fire a fast ball down a bowling alley these days.

But there are some who can tell the story of Bilbow's.

The store at No. 443 where Bilbow's came to its end is taking on new occupants. But the place was vacant and a little helter-skelter the day I went up there looking for one who could tie Bilbow's together.

I found him sitting on a pile of lumber, watching some workmen renovating the place. He came over when I mentioned my mission and together we went down into the basement. To his little work-ship.

And I want to say that Bilbow's—the name—still lives. Bilbow's Billiard Supply Co. is that little workroom down in the basement of No. 443 St. Peter.

The man who runs it is Joe Rongitsch. The last of the billiard table and cue repairmen in the city. Joe kept in operation a form of recreation that has moved from the glamor of the pool hall into the clubs, bowling alleys and basements of private homes.

"I guess there aren't a dozen old-time pool halls left in St. Paul. And there used to be one or two on about every block downtown—not to mention those scattered out into the neighborhoods," said Joe.

There was, however, only one Bilbow's.

"I don't remember now why it was called Bilbow's," said Joe. "When I came there in 1916, Pat Gosewich and Herb Hanch ran it." (Ah, those two names will long ring in billiard history here.)

"I guess it had been going for about six years before I arrived," said Joe. "My shop was there from that day on. Odd, though, I never was much of a billiard player."

There is a picture of Bilbow's that Joe sketched for me that afternoon as we talked in the basement, over the din of the workmen ripping out the last remnants of that famous old pool parlor.

Bilbow's had two rooms of tables—maybe 25 tables in all. (There was a pool hall over in the Hamm building that once had 49.)

"I can see Bilbow's yet," said Joe.

It was the top establishment—the king of them all. Like the Waldorf in New York is to hotels:

Saturday afternoons, and evenings, with the young men—down to their best Sunday vests and trousers, white shirts with ties loose at the open collar, hats on—bending over the green-felted table, while the light from the green, glass cone lampshades beat on the cue ball and the 8 ball.

And spittoons strategically placed and spaced; the racks along the wall; the lunch counter over here; next door the barber shop, separated by a partition.

And the smell of pomade and after-shave lotion mingling with the aromas of sizzling hamburgers, frying on Fred Werden's grill. And roast beef and gravy. Fred was the cook at Bilbow's—lived in the basement.

"He was a great one, that Fred," said Joe. "Boys used to kid him about never leaving the place. Living in the basement. But he'd laugh and say, 'I'll live to visit all of your graves.'

"And Fred was just about right. He was 96 when he died and I guess only a couple of the boys were around."

Bilbow's for 20 or 30 years was the "Corner Drug Store" for the young men of the city, especially the near-loop. They'd come early and stay late—on Saturdays and Sundays.

And by mid-afternoon, the cigar smoke would be hanging up near the ceiling and the light rays cut through like a funnel.

Bilbow's was a meeting place, where youths rendezvoused. And it never took a comic book nor a blonde behind the counter to keep them there. Few women knew Bilbow's and those were a handful of stenographers or store clerks who sometimes played during the noon hour.

"Couple of them were pretty good billiard players," said Joe.

In later years, after Pat Gosewich died, Joe had an interest in the place. And Hy Sigal owned it the last five years.

"Something happened to the popularity of the pool hall," said Joe. "Maybe it was the automobile. Kids always rushing here and there. Thirty years ago they used to come in and play six and eight hours. Maybe shake hooligan or gamble with a punchboard."

Then one by one the old billiard parlors began disappearing from the streets.

"Kids would come in, play for about 30 minutes, then rush off again—nervous, they were," said Joe.

Bilbow's transplant from Minnesota to St. Peter was really an epilogue in its story. Lasted just about a year and a half.

"I'm about all that's left of it," said Joe. "I'm going to stay here in the basement, though, and keep the shop open."

Funny how these things go in the city—an age, an era—rises and falls. And the last chapter is written in the basement of a building on St. Peter Street with a guy named Joe.

The Wreck of Old No. 95

Downtown sidewalk superintendents who have been concentrating so far this summer on supervisory duties in connection with the razing of the Newton block on Minnesota Street have shifted their feet over to 95 E. Kellogg where they will be needed for the next week.

Old No. 95 is coming down, having survived just a little less than a century of progress.

And it is ironical that the building, which once housed the forerunner of the First National Bank, should be torn down by the First National Bank.

If the stately, three-story limestone structure were in the least sensitive about filial devotion, this would certainly be a blow to the pride.

Here this young upstart back a block has the gall to wipe its "Old Dad" from the landscape.

There is a pinch of irony, too, in the fact that No. 95 is making room for a parking lot, a necessity caused by changing times and the fact that the First's new auto bank is just behind it.

At that No. 95 held its ground on what was old Third Street a lot longer than most.

Nobody is now alive who knew the building as the Thompson Brothers Bank. The brothers ended a partnership with the First's founder, Parker Paine, in 1861, to begin their own financial business—Bank of Minnesota.

James Thompson, president, and Horace, cashier, built No. 95 E. Kellogg in 1863 and the charter they were granted was the first national bank charter issued in Minnesota and the territories of Dakota and Montana.

The Thompsons were not alone at No. 95. They occupied only one of three 25-foot sections, one of the others bearing another familiar St. Paul name, the J. L. Forepaugh Co.

Progress already has hacked away all but the bank section, which is the one now being martyred.

I think that about covers the technical background the sidewalk superintendents need to know to perform their jobs effectively.

I hope they are gentle with the old patriarch, when they lower it into the grave.

See you at sidewalk square No. 10 on Kellogg for the last rites. Bring your own handkerchiefs.

Hats Off! The Seven Corners Drugstore Is Passing!

Sam, the news vendor at Seven Corners, pressed his face against the plate glass windows and stared a minute through the empty showcase into the bare room beyond.

"First time in 76 years it's been closed," he said. "Seems like you just figured there'd always be a drugstore here."

The way he kept looking it was as if he half expected some magic spell to suddenly whisk the lipstick and seltzer ads back into the show window, the pretty girl on the poster demonstrating a sunburn lotion, a placard dish of ice cream, topped by a strawberry.

The Seven Corners drugstore is gone. Oldest in the city, starting in 1880. And Sam can't bring it back again—not with all the wishing he does.

There is a void on that once bustling corner that the shopkeepers can't get used to, not in a few days. Nor, for that matter, can the thousands of persons whose paths crisscross on the spot where the front door stands.

For that has been the streetcar and bus transfer point for the city's legions— where east brushed shoulders with west, north nodded to south. The Seven Corners drugstore was the place everybody waited in that mass exchange.

In winter, the crush of people just inside the door at 5 p.m. was like a mob scene, with one self-appointed wayfarer acting as lookout.

"Here comes the St. Clair car," the shout would ring through the store. And for a few minutes a rush of cold, biting air swept in through the open door as the St. Clair riders filed outside.

And in summer—remember how cool the marble counter felt to the touch on a stifling afternoon—the Seven Corners drugstore was a refuge of shade between streetcars. Where you could sit down in the wire-backed chairs, as Joe Nemo remembers it, and revel in the best bittersweet chocolate sundae west of Chicago.

And the old magazine racks—thumbed over by countless hands. Most popular free reading room in town, especially when the Selby-Lake cars were stalled in the tunnel up a few blocks and you had to kill time.

Some days you had to elbow through the "waiting room" to get up to the cigar counter for a package of gum.

But the Seven Corners drugstore was a wonderful place when you ran out of shaving cream, toothpaste, cigarettes or razor blades.

Folks came to rely on it the way they do an old easy chair, or a favorite pair of slippers.

To each of the millions whose steps took them in and out of the store in 76 years, the place holds a special memory.

"The Seven Corners drugstore? Let me tell you about the incident I remember it for," says one man.

"This happened nearly 40 years ago. My wife and I were living up on Sixth Street. She was expecting our first child. One night she called—I was working nights then—and said I better come home right away. So I did and hired a cab and we drove to the hospital. But it was a false alarm. She went home.

"Next night she called. I went home, but not quite so fast. And we didn't go to Ancker hospital in a cab. No sir. We walked down the hill, climbed on the stools in the Seven Corners drugstore and had a leisurely ice cream soda. Then we got on the streetcar and went to the hospital. I'll never forget the drugstore."

It was the anchor of the Moore block, in more illustrious years the medical center of the city. S. H. Reeves, it was, who opened up on the corner in 1880, then came Henry McCall, former city councilman, and after him, I believe, Ed Seiberlich and at the end Edmund Oelke.

It was a stepping stone for Mr. Seiberlich, who went on to become president of Northwestern Drug Co. And during his reign one peculiar thing. For 19 years, day or night, when you walked into the place, there was one of the Kulisheck boys on duty. Maybe it was Joe, Art or Adolph. But the last name behind the counter was Kulisheck.

I guess not even the rumors could convince the people on the Corners that the drugstore would close.

"I came here years ago," says Mario Nardi who runs a cafe next to the old drugstore. "If you ever told me I'd see the day when that place would be empty I would have said you were crazy."

And there's something a little forlorn about watching Sam, the news vendor on the corner for 14 years, standing there in silent mourning, trying in vain as he peers through the window, to bring back time.

World's Biggest Indian

Charles Meehan of 476 Brimhall is something of a Johnny-come-lately to the St. Paul scene, but in the space of a very short time he has become, perhaps the outstanding authority on one of the city's principal statuary works—the Courthouse Indian.

This piece of sculpture, 36 feet tall, done in Mexican onyx, cost $80,000 at the time of presentation in May of 1936 and is dedicated to the memory of city and county war veterans.

Its creator, Carl Milles, called it The God of Peace.

Here Mr. Meehan, who has studied this thing from all angles, takes some issue with the portrayal of the massive Indian, and the legend posted near the base.

While the legend suggests a group of Indians, smoking their pipe of peace at the base, and the smoke rising into the form of an Indian god of peace, Mr. Meehan observes that the Indian may also be viewed in a somewhat different manner.

"The hand which in legend is said to be 'extended in a gesture of friendliness' rather appears posed in some form of military salute," he says. "Also, the pipe of peace is held close to the body and the position of the supporting hand suggests a soldier bearing a shouldered rifle."

Now, Mr. Meehan does not take exception to the ideals exemplified by the Indian, but he does point out that the headdress worn by the Indian is commonly known in Indian circles as a war bonnet.

"Thus we can conclude," says Mr. Meehan, "that the work shows that peace is not alone the absence of war, but more importantly a state of mind."

You can smoke a pipe of peace over that awhile.

Mr. Meehan's interest in the Indian stems, he says, from the visit an aunt of his made a few years ago to the points of interest in the city. When she had seen the Indian, she asked for a souvenir of it to take back to her home.

There was none to be had. This gave her nephew an idea that visitors to the city hall ought to have a souvenir Indian if they wished and he arranged with a local sculptress, Evelyn Peabody, to make a model.

About 500 such souvenir Indians have been distributed free to visitors by the mayor's office in lieu of the key to the city.

The Indian, Mr. Meehan says, kind of grows on you.

[*Since this has been written, the City Hall Indian has become a major tourist attraction. Nicknamed Onyx John, it was officially renamed "Vision of Peace" in 1995.*]

Ring the Bell at 216 Indiana

The three houses stand at No. 196, 200 and 216 W. Indiana, on the West Side, set against the sandstone cliffs like an Alpine village.

The houses are weathered and solid-looking like gnarled oaks; they are fringed around the edges in an old world style of architecture. But that is not what makes you take a second look.

It's the mosaic art work inlaid in panels across the fronts. No. 216 is the big house with the more elaborate mosaic touches. Here is where the idea must have begun. "You go back there and ring the bell. They know about it," says the woman who comes to the screen door of the big house.

"Back there" is a wooden building looking like an ancient machine shop, set flush against the foot of the sheer rock hill.

In this business you learn that the unexpected comes when you least expect it. You learn that in a city can be many things.

You want proof? Ring the bell at the old machine shop, behind 216 Indiana, and inquire about who designed the mosaic panels for the houses on the street and why.

The bell brings a man around the corner of the shop. "Ah, yes, the mosaic," he says. "That was done by my grandfather—Paul Ferodowill. Owned the entire block at one time," says the grandson, Eugene J. Ferodowill.

"Liked a Bavarian touch about his architecture. He was a contractor, you know. That's Persian mosaic. Done with old bits of broken glass and dishes. Grandfather built all three houses."

It would be easy now to thank Mr. Ferodowill and leave. "I've got a little shop back in here now," he says. "Maybe you'd like to see it."

You cross the threshold, out of the abnormally hot sun, and walk into the city's first, last and only completely air-conditioned building by nature's own system—cold air pouring out of the caves in the sandstone hillside.

"I'm not so much for machinery," I tell him.

"We make ice skate sharpening equipment here," he says. And modestly he starts to describe one of the fascinating little industries, spawned in St. Paul, nourished by worldwide demand and which scarcely a soul in town knows exists. Unless you are in the market for ice skate sharpening equipment.

But the cast of "Ice Capades" are and also "Holiday on Ice." And Sonja Henie's troupe.

Because the "Ferrodowill Skate Sharpening Co." (they use two Rs in the trademark name) is one of two such in the world, and the largest.

Eugene's father, Joseph, invented the sharpeners and skate holders. Joseph was a remarkable man in other ways, too.

At the rear of the shop he built a storeroom, using for the walls old, hard rubber truck tires, cemented together. Undoubtedly the only walls of their kind in the world.

Joseph Ferodowill—he died several years ago—also dabbled in aviation. At the age of 15 he drew a sketch ("Entirely from Emagination" it says) of a dirigible powered by helicopter-like blades, set on top. His model still stands on a shelf, gathering dust.

So you leave Mr. Ferodowill's naturally air-cooled machine shop and go back to the street.

And take another look at the mosaic panels on the three houses which is why you stopped to talk to Mr. Ferodowill in the first place.

A city like St. Paul is full of the unexpected—especially there on Indiana Street.

[*The Ferodowill house was razed in 1966.*]

Booya, Boo-ya, Booya, Boo-ya

As regards the gastronomic life of the city, let me say that we are all fortunate to be eating in St. Paul.

Because when it comes to following closely the fashions and fads in cookery, our cooks not only equal the rest of the nation—they improve upon the original.

Our chow mein, barbecued ribs, pizza, spaghetti and even smorgasbords are unsurpassed, whether you eat them in the formality of a hotel or cafe dining room, or in the kitchen of the house down the street, the church basement or fire hall.

We may not have invented any of these dishes, but St. Paul cooks certainly have given them new zest and distinctiveness. And I have eaten whereof I speak.

But there is one dish which I have purposely saved for special mention because I don't think it has been given proper dignity, nor do we take proper credit for its presentation.

This is the booya.

It is as difficult to define the contents of the booya as it is the word. I have always said that a booya consists of anything worth eating, and everything.

And while, from a point of hygiene, a booya probably should consist only of rather domestic-type foods, there are those old-timers around town who lament the fact that tiled kitchens, gas stoves and so on have taken the kick out of the long ago booyas, cooked over a blazing wood fire.

When a few embers, ashes, dead flies and mosquitoes did not detract, but added to the over-all effect.

I don't suppose there is a single food fashion that taxes the endurance and courage of its cooks as much as booya. Once it's in the pot and the fire's lit, brother, you've got to keep stirring and adding until it's done. And it requires muscle to keep those paddles pushing the pottage.

This is something that lasts more than 12 hours.

We could argue all night about how long it takes to cook a good booya, or about who invented it and where, in St. Paul, you get the best.

West Side booyas have their special devotees; in the north end, booya has hundreds of fans. Fire departments and Legion and VFW posts the county over—also churches—undoubtedly stir up huge cauldrons of fine tasting stuff.

But the heart of "Booyaland" in St. Paul, that neighborhood of fine folks of Czech and Polish descent, seems to be out in the West End, in the district around Randolph and W. Seventh.

And modest as they are, few will dispute their claim that the modern booya as we eat it today, nationwide, may well have had its inception in the backyard pots of the West End.

Thus it was that the other dark and rainy Saturday about midnight, I adjourned to the Ran-View VFW (Post 6210) club at 698 Stewart, to watch the preparation—ritual—of a rather traditional booya.

Here, I had been told, were incorporated all the ingredients, techniques and arts of the finest booyas, a formula developed long ago by Dan Vogelgesang, who used to run a bar on Randolph and verbally passed on the recipe.

"It is legend," whispered Louis Bertrand, "that Dan's formula was unsurpassed."

Louis and the others were in the clubrooms taking a coffee break when I arrived. And a little discouraged I hadn't got in on the very beginning—which began at 7 p.m. that Saturday, with the shredding and slicing of the vegetables, the unloading of the boxes of oxtails, chunks of veal, beef, beef and veal bones.

As Bill Landshut explained it, the ordering is done well in advance, by calling a certain food market in the area and saying: "Listen, we're going to have a booya at the club Sunday." That code phrase is sufficient to send the food store into action and they just load it into the truck on "Booya Eve."

The boys had just got the fires going and the pots—full of beef and veal bones—simmering when I got there.

About 15 minutes later, we all moved en masse out the back door to the only booya shack, privately owned, in the city.

Though the night was dark, my nose led me directly to the building, set behind the clubhouse. A wall fan already was sending the heady booya fumes and steam into the darkness.

This form of advertisement has sometimes brought uninvited guests to help stand "the booya watch" through the night. Mr. Landshut and Paul Johnson recalled, I believe, the "uninvited" passerby who brought a bottle of whisky to help tide him through the rigors of night and, in a moment of enthusiasm, dumped the contents into the booya pot. "It was too late to start a new pot," said Mr. Landshut, "so we just served it as is."

The Ran-View booya shack is a remarkable place, with a long brick counter running the length of one side and set into it two huge cauldrons, about 4 to 5 feet in diameter, and fired from below by gas burners.

Heady steam was already filling the place, with warm fragrant humidity, when we walked in. One cauldron was bubbling. Mr. Landshut or maybe it was Dick Paulson, was pouring water into the second, using a hose.

A policeman, off duty but in uniform, stood guard at the door. For in booya circles, the competition is as keen as that between Chrysler and General Motors, and spies are a constant problem.

"You understand," said Mr. Johnson, "that from now until Sunday at noon, we got to keep stirring. And everything goes in according to schedule."

Standing in big pots on the floor were cut potatoes, carrots, onions, shredded cabbage, even a bowl of peeled garlic, beans, two pints and four half pints of Worcestershire sauce, cans of corn, tomatoes, boxes of dressed chickens, veal, beef, even some smoked ham hocks.

While we talked, comrades Paulson, Johnson, Landshut, Bertrand stirred the bubbling liquid with big paddles.

"Here, you take a turn," said one of them. And so I stirred the bones around for about 20 minutes.

Come noon Sunday, the shack would be a busy place as booya fans assembled, pails and pots in hand, to get their booya—one big dipper for 35 cents.

"We gotta metal lamp shade with a hole in the end to use as a funnel to fill bottles with booya," said Mr. Landshut. Some take their booya home, others eat it right at the club. Any left over goes to St. Joseph's Children's home.

I stayed around until 2 a.m. when they put the oxtails in the pots. Out of deference to my honest face, they did not search me and their trust is justified. I did not steal the formula.

Through the City

Island in the City

I suppose that if Williams Hill reminds you of anything at all, it would be a tiny kingdom, set in the heart of the city, surrounded by a moat of railroad tracks.

I first saw the place on a bleak November's day a few years ago when I was driving out Mississippi street, through that fabled section of St. Paul called Lowertown.

I turned where the sign reads Williams Street and went across the quaint, little wooden bridge, spanning a track, and was reminded of a drawbridge leading to some ancient castle.

But I had picked the wrong season of the year to really enjoy the wonders of Williams Hill. For summer—when the sun is warm and the birds in good voice—is the time to explore Williams Hill and its little paths and forests—right there in the heart of the railroad yards.

I went back there the other day, just on a hunch, and was struck by the timelessness of the little island.

For all around it the city has changed—the old houses ripped out in the area that looks west to the Capitol. New buildings are going up on the Mt. Airy peak not far away. And the new highway building has risen above the skyline.

But Williams Hill is not much removed from the way its settlers left it nearly 80 years ago, abandoning that kingdom for Summit Avenue and Mounds Boulevard and the fields beyond.

The fire hydrants are still there, if you part the weeds; so are the cobblestone gutters, running along the old streets and roads—now rough with sharp rocks and boulders. Sidewalks still run up Williams Street, though time has crumbled them in places. But the three or four houses still remaining are cloaked from the city's sight by massive trees and broad, green lawns sweep from the doorstoops to the road.

If you follow the trail down the east side of the hill, you pass the hollow shells of two houses, all but disintegrated. At the peak of Williams Street, where you reach the summit of the hill, is a home once said to have belonged to the Norwegian consul.

And who knows the ruins of houses, belonging to grander years, buried under the brush and sod? There are some. For Williams Hill, in the 1870s, was the summit of the social ladder; below the hill along Broadway and Lafayette road lived those in more mundane surroundings.

There are two marvels on Williams Hill for the visitor: the view of the city and the strange feeling you have, hiking through one of the little forests in the center, sliced by rutted trails, heavy with brush and thickets, filled with varieties of birds and woodland animals and marred only by occasional evidence of civilization—piles of empty tin cans and ashes from campfires.

You could just as well be 200 miles away from the sight of the First National bank building. And it is a little shocking to emerge from the woods and remember, suddenly, that you are—after all— less than a half mile from the heart of the loop; that only a bridge separates you from urban life and that those voices echoing faintly from below are railroad crewmen switching passenger cars at the Great Northern coach yards.

It may seem incongruous that when you mention the place, so many thousands will say: "And where is Williams Hill?"

Or they will recall its shameful notoriety of a few years back when a little boy was found murdered just under the wooden bridge. You remember the "O'Brien murder case"? That gave the place a quality of shivery mystery.

I am somewhat relieved to find that there are no present plans in city hall or at the highway department to do more than take a slice off the north side of the hill for fill.

[*By 1999 Williams Hill became a part of the city's Phalen Corridor Initiative and faced a future as an industrial park.*]

Fabulous Hill Street

You walk down Hill Street from Kellogg, and the Ramsey county morgue stands where it did then. Across the street is a parking lot run by the city, and a lone elm tree.

And at midnight the street is as quiet as—well, as the morgue—and unless you remembered or had heard, there is nothing to give away the fabulous and hitherto unpublished story of the era when Hill Street was the "Business man's Barbary Coast."

But the tales of what went on there are still told from the lips of men who knew its inner secrets and the rest who heard the stories and pass them along.

Some are true and some have been embroidered. But of this there is no question: There was never a street in the city like Hill between 1890 and the mid-1920s. And hopefully there never will be again.

Let me set the scene: The morgue, and at 222 Eagle, on the corner of Eagle and Hill, was Mamie Porter's Chicken Shack and, kitty-corner, the Bucket of Blood saloon.

Lining the block opposite the morgue were the houses of such as Dottie Hazzard, Marie Dairfax, and the most widely known of them all—Nina Clifford's at 147 Hill.

These were night clubs, with their 1900 version of B-girl entertainers.

Up above, looking down at it all from Third Street and Washington, was Central Police Station.

They were open 24 hours a day, except for Sunday and Mondays when the club operators dressed their hostesses up in conservative, black finery with more fashion than the Summit carriage trade could boast.

Mamie Porter's Chicken Shack was the gastronomical star of Hill Street. Her fried chicken was like nothing else in this world before or since. This I have from some of her former customers, whose mouths still water when they tell about it. Mamie fried her chicken in pure butter and you came in and sat at white, wood counters and waited 30 or 40 minutes for your chicken to be cooked to order. It was a favorite rendezvous for taxicabs and horse-drawn hacks because Mamie's chicken drew patrons from near and far and the later the hour—or earlier—the better was business.

The clubs and resorts that lined the street were noted for luxury. Heavy and colorful draperies, low-hanging prism-glass chandeliers, and Victorian overstuffed settees were the rule. Plushness throughout, starting with their carved doorways and down the carpeted stairways.

The "Hill Street stories" are legion.

There was the chauffeur for one of the mayors who, as a prank, used to delight in parking the official car down on Hill Street until his honor at last appealed to him, in view of the forthcoming election, to cease.

And there were rumors, never confirmed, that one candidate for the presidency of the Minnesota club—just above Hill Street—ran on the platform of promising to dig a tunnel from the club basement into one of the Hill Street places. It was never dug.

The operators of these night spots were all well-known, but the most famous was Nina Clifford.

Hers was a red-brick house, set back a little from the street. And the plat maps show that it was built in 1888.

Nina—that wasn't her real name—will always be remembered for her great generosity.

There is the story about the man, on his uppers, who went to her back door one day and asked for a job. She offered him one as an accountant, but he knew nothing about bookkeeping.

So Nina gave him a dollar, which he used to purchase some oranges. These he sold and bought some more—and finally parlayed that dollar into a prosperous business. There are other sagas of loans she made to keep businesses and corporations running.

But the all-time legend of Nina Clifford came after her death. As news of her passing (she was in her 80s) spread, a few men decided to perpetrate a fantastic practical joke.

Reaching for telephones, they began calling leading business and civic leaders of the day. To each they said in their best mourning tones:

"It is with regret that we inform you Nina Clifford has just died. In going through her effects, the undertaker discovered a letter from her in which she made one last request that you serve as one of the pallbearers at her funeral."

On the day of her funeral, there was a sudden mass exodus of prominent men out of the city on "business trips," the story goes.

Not one of the men called showed up, but many of their wives did to see whose husbands would be there.

The old red-brick house at 147 Hill—right under the Kellogg underpass—survived a few more years. For a brief time, after the repeal of prohibition, it was operated as a tavern. And then, on Oct. 19, 1937, the *Dispatch* noted:

"What death and taxes began on the once notorious establishment of Nina Clifford, the WPA is destined to finish." A court order had directed the house be torn down because of long overdue taxes and the crumbling condition of the building.

So crumbled, too, the last remnant of a gay street and one of the more unsavory chapters of St. Paul's growing pains.

Yet, if you want the true shades of color in a city's history, it is a story that is long overdue in the telling.

The Barton-Omaha Colony

At heart, I think I am a collector. Not of coins or stamps or matchbook covers. But odd neighborhoods, strange little cloisters in the city.

Sometimes when I find one, I feel a bit guilty. Because once exposed in print, they lose some of the intrigue and charm that fascinated me in the first place.

Like the quaint nest of houses, set back under the shelf of the sandstone cliffs, just up from the Mississippi near the Omaha railway trestle on the city's West End.

Actually I do not feel badly about examining this completely hidden section of the city in public. Some day, when Shepard road strikes on west beyond the foot of the James Street hill, the highway will skirt the bluff directly above the neighborhood I am describing. (In fact, residents there are worrying about cars careening over the edge onto their roofs.)

Even now, the only access to the Barton-Omaha street colony is along the Upper Levee road, to be known as Shepard. Out of the Loop, past the Northern States Power coal docks, along the inlet where, on the dune across the water, the neighborhood youngsters build fires to dry their clothes, wet from swimming.

Just before the roadway reaches the Omaha mainline crossing—you take a sharp left, at the sign which reads: Richmond.

Richmond drops, a dusty, potholed road, downhill, alongside the tracks, then turns right and under a trestle.

But now you are no longer on Richmond. You have just entered Omaha. Only then do you see the colony of houses, all lining the slopes up to the cliff wall.

The fence gates, barns, sheds, one with a fading sign which says: "Beware of Dog."

The neat gardens where the bean and pea shoots are arranged in neat rows and the staked-up tomato plants are budding with yellow blossoms.

The terraced yard, filled with gay colors, mixtures of flowers, iris, petunias, geraniums and herds of wooden animals stuck into the ground.

Without knowing it, you leave Omaha street and enter Barton. Same crooked, ambling, rock-ribbed street. But the name changes at about No. 478 Barton.

This is the home of Mrs. Robert Fischbach.

"I don't know why the street name changes at the edge of my property," she says. "All I know is that this is so."

Mrs. Fischbach, or her family, rank among the pioneers of the Omaha-Barton street colony.

"I guess we have lived here maybe 40 years or more," she says. "We're not exactly early settlers. Squatters might be a better name."

Mrs. Fischbach doesn't think about it much, but she and all the other dozen or so families in the colony live on the most historic piece of ground in the city.

Because, somewhere through that glen, about a block away and up the cliffside is Fountain cave, where St. Paul began.

That was where Pierre (Pig's Eye) Parrant set up his whisky shop so long ago and founded the town.

"I guess it is up there," she says, "the entrance is covered, they say. But we use our own caves."

And here is something distinctive about life on Omaha-Barton Street—each house is equipped with a cave.

Mrs. Fischbach led me around the back of her home to the Fischbach cave—once used to store food.

The entrance is supported by a wooden frame and when she opened the old door, you could feel the cold air.

"Don't use it now much," she says. "I've still got a few canned goods in there, but not much."

I submit that you can go up on Edgcumbe Boulevard, past the multi-thousand-dollar homes and not find a one with a natural air-conditioned room, walk-in cooler, also easily converted into a bomb shelter. But these luxuries are old hat down on Omaha-Barton street. Had 'em for years.

Another thing about living down under the cliff is the easy winters.

"Wind just kind of blows over us," says Mrs. Fischbach. "Spring comes early." And I looked in the direction she was pointing and I saw the view of the far side of the river valley, a choice view.

"But," she says, "we have no sewer, no water."

And I noticed that across the road, people have been dumping refuse, cans, bottles, old lumber—not residents on the street—but interlopers.

"Then we had the floods back a few years, too," she says. "Water came up above your head where you're standing.

"We just went out the back door which is higher," she says.

I left Mrs. Fischbach and drove on down the road, which dribbles away into an adventuresome trail for another two blocks, ending at the riverside and the pipeline crossing.

Here the houses give way to dense brush and forest, but the landscape is marred by human garbage and rubbish. The car retraced the street, past the old, red shed with initials and dates, going back to 1921, carved on one side.

Back under the trestle again. Look behind and you'd swear there wasn't a thing, except swamp, where that road turns.

Cave City

The west side cliffs curve with majesty off Channel Street at Wabasha and work their way gradually westward toward Ole Miss and like a big, shaggy step they parallel the river for two miles to a point just under the Omaha railway bridge.

And in the shadow, at the bottom of the step, runs Water Street. When Ole Miss behaves, Water is a lazy, river town road, quite out of character in the metropolis. And when the river is rampaging, Water lives up to its name.

Back toward Wabasha, at the sweep of the cliffs, Indiana Street becomes like Water, lying in the mountainous shadows. And the sometimes lethargic, tranquil, off-beat character of the area is as misleading as silver plating on a gold spoon. For this is the neighborhood of the caves, where a whole economy and countless legends lie locked from view inside those rustic cliffs.

Nearly everybody who lives at the foot of the cliffs owns his own cave. As you drive along Water, you see the wood entrances. And if you look far on top of the cliffs, you will see little air vents. Some caves run only a few dozen feet into the cliffside and hold such things as canned goods, potatoes and family provisions—for temperatures in the West Side caves never vary much from 40 to 50 degrees, summer and winter.

And some of the caves are huge labyrinths, buildings, of two levels, thousands of square feet, fingers probing deep under the West Side. One cave begins at 442 Water and runs in a horseshoe through the bowels of the hill, emerging several blocks away, near the High Bridge.

For the householder, who has no basement, the cave is an excellent substitute. But the caves have played stranger roles.

This dark, dark cave city of giant-sized rooms was man-made in the beginning, its limestone sand feeding the foundries that built and glassed-in the city.

Pickmarks of those pioneer laborers still cut herringbone patterns in the arched ceilings. There are caves of glamor and magnificence. Once, in the 1930s, the West Side caves spawned one of the oddest night club belts in the world.

First there was just the "Cave." Its popularity sprouted the Mystic Cavern, up near the Omaha bridge, and then William

Lehmann, the Mushroom King, built the fabulous Castle Royal at Wabasha and Channel, in 1931.

"Yes, Sir," said Joe Altendorfer, one of three big mushroom growers on Water Street, "I can look down at Water Street there now and still see the bumper-to-bumper cars that poured past here day and night to those nightclubs. Dust got so bad the city finally oiled the street."

They're storing potatoes now in the old Mystic Cavern. And Land O'Lakes ages cheese in the Castle Royal. But the famed Castle is still almost like it was the night William Lehmann closed it back in 1940—the castle-like exterior trim, the big dance floor, the $4,300, 24-karat gold chandeliers that came from the old Gates mansion in Minneapolis—the exquisite water fountain at the entrance to the main dining room—the stippled walls of bronzed gold—these are all there. Catering now to huge wheels of red, black and yellow-wax cheeses on racks.

And next door, Mr. Lehmann, busy packing mushrooms, paused to reminisce a little. About how it was when the Castle was open from dusk to dawn and cars jammed the parking lot the night Cab Calloway's band played to a cheering audience.

"Was never a piece of meat came out of the kitchen that it didn't have mushrooms on it," said Mr. Lehmann. And the Castle introduced the popular 1930 delicacy—sliced mushroom sandwiches.

There are those on Water and Channel and Indiana Streets who lament the passing of the night club era in the caves. "This could have been the most popular entertainment center in the Northwest," they said.

Instead it became the locale of the largest mushroom business west of Chicago. A man named Peltier and his French-Canadian neighbors first discovered you could grow mushrooms in the caves back in the 1880s. There was also a man named Mushnot, who was a pioneer mushroomer. At one time 11 growers lined the cliffs from Channel to Twin City Brick.

There are other caves of legend though. Some now closed which housed illicit stills and stabled horses. One through which a spring flowed. And another, now closed, covering 20,000 square feet, built like a tree, with a trunk and branches, running under Chippewa Avenue near Baker.

Excellent bomb shelters, storage depots? There was talk in World War II about such uses, real estateman George Benz recalls. The walls and floors are hard as cement. But in dry heat, they begin to crumble.

Go over to old Yoerg's Brewery, now owned by the Harris Plumbing Co., and Ronnie Harris and Sheldon Stewart will guide you through the two-story Yoerg caves, where not long after 1848, barrels of widely-drunk Yoerg's beer were cave-aged. Now the cave building houses plumbing supplies, in those high-ceilinged vaults, from which hang bats like black blobs.

So you leave this strange underground city and go down Water Street, deceptively casual and quaint.

And reflect on the romance of a city which holds a little community, sustained for three quarters of a century by picturesque, towering cliffs, whose striped sides look like gold in the late afternoon sun.

Where the Crocus Blooms

You can hardly see the hillside now for the foliage and trees that have grown up there. But a long time ago, when the city was new, the first rays of the May sun caught the hillside and warmed it. And the wild crocus grew.

Looking up from their homes that stretched to the river's bank, in such neighborhoods as Irvine Park and the old Fort Road, residents viewed the blooming sight appreciatively and gave the hill a name.

They called it Crocus Hill, and so it has remained through the eras of time and the city, a little appendix-like street and square at the end of Goodrich and not far from Dale, strolling off into a tinier and placid place called Kenwood Parkway.

Crocus Hill and Crocus Place have aged and prospered and become a residential haven for affluent and gentle folks, who admire big lawns and the quiet shade of an elm on a still, hot summer's afternoon.

There are, too, the majestic views of the valley below when autumn paints the terraces red, gold and orange. Then, as the leaves drop away, the setting opens to an incomparable panorama of the city at winter; the High Bridge like a string of moving lights at night and West Seventh looking Christmasy with its vari-colored signs and blue-white street lights stretching along the valley floor.

All these spectacles have endeared Crocus Hill and Place to its residents. But more than the view, I suspect, has been the delicious feeling of being tucked completely away from the rest of the city. The stranger never locates either. He bumbles into them and leaves by trial and error.

Crocus Hill begins rather arbitrarily in the middle of a block. You are driving on Goodrich when suddenly it has become Crocus Hill. Nor are the house numbers any help at all. They follow no logical sequence.

One explanation offered is that numbers were selected on a first come basis. The possessors of No. 1 are the John C. Cornings. No. 3 is now in between occupants and is known as the Adams house, having been built by a man named John Quincy Adams, no less. Next door is No. 8, the home of Dr. Marguerite Schwyzer, whose late father was one of the city's first names in medical history.

No. 2 Crocus Hill is at the end of the block, the dead end, far from 3 or 5 or 8 and is the Bill Lang home, one of the most striking residences in the city. And well worth a trip to see, even from the exterior.

While I may be maligning all the rest by picking out one for more careful examination, I was charmed by the big, old, sedate mansion at No. 4 and the lady who lives there. The house, with its canopied entrance, driveway winding under and through the spacious grounds, exiting on the street at the rear. And its owner, Mrs. C. W. Stott, a Saunders girl who married the man that made Stott Briquets famous.

The graciousness of both house and owner complement each other. Mrs. Stott has lived through only a portion of the old home's history. A total of 35 years. Before that it was lived in for some 25 years by a family named Baer. Earlier than that it was the temporary residence of Gov. Merriam who moved in after his home burned across from the State Capitol. Even before that, the house was known as the Crocus Hill club.

"All told," said Mrs. Stott, "we have traced it back into its 80th year, more or less. It was built by a man who never lived in it."

As evidence of its patriarchal status on Crocus Hill, No. 4 stands on a commanding location—one side looking across the lawn to the brow of the terraces dropping down the name-sake hill to Pleasant Avenue. Its front door peers across a little square. At the back are more lawns with flower borders.

Mrs. Stott wears no airs about her role as an historian of Crocus Hill and Place. In fact she modestly apologized for not being able to be of more help. Yet, standing in front of her home, she can point around the ridge which is Crocus Place to homes of such illustrious neighbors as Louis W. Hill Jr., grandson of the Empire Builder, and Athelstan Spilhaus, head of the University of Minnesota Institute of Technology.

"That beautiful home across the street," she recalled, "was built of stone taken from buildings that were wrecked along old Third Street when it was converted into Kellogg Boulevard. Mrs. David Aberle lives there."

And one of the reasons Mr. Stott moved to No. 4 Crocus Hill was to be near Mrs. Stott's aunt, Mrs. Charles Morris, at 613 Goodrich, at the boundary of Crocus Hill. Mr. Morris was the architect and engineer for the Duluth aerial bridge and the St. Paul High Bridge.

One must mention, too, such neighbors as Mrs. Horace Thompson and Mrs. Arthur Savage, both widely-known St. Paul names. The late Dr. John S. Abbott, C. W. Griggs and T. R. O'Brien on Crocus Place. Investment man Harold Wood at 12 Crocus Hill. Charles L. Sommers at 7.

Long before Crocus Hill reached its true stature, it played a part in city lore. James Wickes Taylor, American consul at Winnipeg from 1870 to 1893, lived on Irvine Park within view of Crocus Hill. Each spring he would go to the hill and gather bouquets which he gave to his friends. After his death, his portrait was hung in the old Winnipeg city hall and each spring, in May, a bouquet of crocuses was placed under it.

In fact that little tribute from Canadians to an American may still be observed in present times. A delightful sidelight to a delightful part of the city.

Iris Lake and the Remnants of a Dream

It lies like a tiny oasis in the desert of commerce. A lake called Iris. In the Midway district hard by University Avenue where, day in day out, thousands pass.

A few are lucky and sit on the benches at the noon hour and eat their lunches or rest in the late afternoon sun and feed the squirrels.

But always, on the shore of the lake, there is that low, raucous rush of roaring traffic sounding in the background, from University Avenue, as it sweeps between Prior and Fairview, which bracket the lake and the park that once sprawled south to the Short Line tracks.

And if still you haven't located it in your mind, let me be even simpler. Go east on University from Prior and one block beyond and to your right—on Lynnhurst or Iris Place.

Iris isn't much of a lake now, but then it never was. I doubt that a boat was ever floated on its waters, yet it is a scenic little body of water—in wet years and a damp basin in the dry years.

Great trees ring the lake and partly hide the broad front lawns and spacious homes. And it is a pleasant interlude to wind through the twisting streets in that maze—Feronia, Oakley.

On Feronia is, appropriately, the Feronia hotel, with bachelor apartments mostly. And the big mansion at 1879 Feronia, with its screened-in porch, is part of the Episcopal Home of Minnesota. It was built by John G. Hinkel in the 1880s.

The home and the lake and the winding lanes are all that remain of a dream that belonged to Mr. Hinkel and Herman Grote. It was a dream called Union Park, covering 33 acres, bounded by University, Prior, Fairview and the tracks. In the dream was an amusement park.

Some parts of the fantasy became real. In 1880 the Milwaukee had just finished the Short Line between the Twin Cities. Union Park was outside the city limits of St. Paul, a wilderness of low, wooded hills.

Merriam Park station provided an excellent entree to the park from either city. A natural park site, it seemed then to Messrs. Grote and Hinkel.

On the University Avenue side of the lake was erected an arched gate and near the center of the park, just south of Lake Iris, was a dance pavilion, with adjoining bandstand. There were refreshment booths spotted here and there and even a merry-go-round. Not far from the pavilion the men put in a bowling alley and an 85-foot observation tower.

Union Park and Lake Iris were at their peak in the summer of 1883. That was the summer when Siebert's Great Western band played on Sundays. A lady named Mlle. Lottie St. Clair made balloon ascensions every afternoon and the Charest family performed daring feats on the high wire.

Thousands strolled the grounds, enjoying the festivities which were cheap even by 1883 standards—15 cents for the roundtrip train ride and a quarter to get into the park, which was protected against freeloaders by a high, wood fence.

But Union Park remained to amuse citizens of two cities only briefly. When Mr. Grote sold his share to Mr. Hinkel in the fall of 1883, Mr. Hinkel was seized with foresight even beyond the idea of an amusement park. He began platting the park for home sites, laying out the streets to follow the natural vales and hills around the lake.

Except that you know how it was once, it would take a wild imagination to believe that this seasoned, old residential niche in the city—quiet, peaceful—ever had such beginnings.

But if Mr. Hinkel's original venture was short-lived, his second guess has stood the test of time. Because, though Lake Iris is surrounded by commercial fever, it still is a place where the frenzied urbanite can turn out of the traffic pressure and luxuriate on a park bench.

Unfortunately, most of them are so engrossed in fighting through the maelstrom of machines that they never even see this haven.

45th Parallel Half Way to the Pole

Two hundred feet north of Roselawn Avenue on Cleveland in Ramsey County, just to the right of the road, is a monument which marks one of the world's unusual geographical locations.

If you stand next to the plate, you will be, at that point, exactly half way between the equator and the North Pole.

The plaque reads:

"This plate marks a point on the 45th parallel of north latitude which is an east-west line on the surface of the earth exactly half the distance from the equator to the North pole. A distance of 3,102 miles each way."

This discovery and its unusual aspects were made back in 1940 by Harry Bronson, at present the Ramsey county engineer and then county surveyor.

"I had known for some time, of course, that the 45th parallel was around there some place," he says. "But it wasn't until then that I got the idea to pin it down exactly."

Harry took a sextant out to the area and found the line, which he marked on N. Cleveland on the west end of the county, and near the tool shed of Keller golf course, on the east end.

"For some reason it gave me a little thrill when I located the points," he says.

Just as it must have the thousands of persons who have paused, stopped, read, then stood next to the monument. Even in the winter, footprints in the snow testify to the attraction the place has for visitors.

And those residents who live on the north side of Roselawn Avenue, or its extensions which are County Road A2 and, further east, Frost Avenue, can say quite airily and accurately when asked their address:

"Oh, we live half way between the equator and the North pole."

Alma Mater Over into Minneapolis

Some one day in the early autumn when the leaves are turning and the night falls in a crisp, chilly blanket across the knoll, I like to go back to the campus I knew not so long ago.

For me it is the University of Minnesota.

And, as I walk the mall from Coffman Union to Northrop, I remember my freshman week back in 1939 and the tingles that ran up my spine when, as the Class of '43 met for the first time, we sang the "Minnesota Rouser" in the big auditorium. And watched the bonfire's glow on the parade near Fourth Street on the night before the first football game.

So I cross the mall and turn toward the massive Memorial stadium, empty and bright in the fall sunshine.

And I remember that November afternoon in 1940, with the cold drizzle falling, when I sat on the sidelines as a cub reporter and watched Bruce Smith of Minnesota fight it out with Tommy Harmon of Michigan for the "Little Brown Jug." And Minnesota won, 7 to 6.

Those were the days of the Golden Gophers when they were a sight to see, racing onto the field, clad in gold helmets, pants and jerseys, a golden horde.

So I cross near old Pillsbury hall and go back to the days of the journalism school when Max Shulman and Tom Heggen were the literary stalwarts even then and Max used to hold court in the old Ski-U-Mah office at noon, the aroma of salami sandwiches choking the atmosphere.

Max went on to the big time and so did Tom, though he died as strangely as he lived, but not before writing "Mr. Roberts."

And I walk down fraternity row and see the young fellows sunning on the front porches and down on sorority row, around Tenth Street, I smile to remember the day I spent in the Pi Phi house as a reporter and how we used to crowd the vestibule of the Alpha Chi Omega house with couples late on Saturday nights. It was more like Grand Central station than a sorority house entry. But nobody seemed to mind.

And how, on those cold, winter's nights, you and your best girl longed for the day when you might have a warm room, at least to say "goodnight." And you talked about tomorrow's coke date at the Varsity cafe and only vaguely of the distant tomorrows because there was a war out there somewhere to win. And you wondered what would happen.

I go down Washington past the old Harvard Grill where, to relieve the tension, we used to meet on football eves and carve our initials into the table tops and the walls would rock to the cheers and voices raised in "I Had A Dream," "You Are My Sunshine," and "Sweetheart of Sigma Chi."

And the Union—ah, I remember the day in 1940 when I went through its partly constructed skeleton and marveled at the dimensions.

That place was a tradition even before it was two years old. My class made history there at Thanksgiving of 1940 when we took off our shoes at twilight dances and electrified the nation with "Shoeless Dancing" and old "Dean Nick" tsk tsked for a week.

I peer into the grand ballroom and my mind flashes back to the afternoon in 1942 when Dimitri Mitropoulos, Minneapolis Symphony conductor, sat cross-legged on the floor and beat time with his hands as the Pettifords et al., beat out the premier performance of "Beat Me Dimitri," eight to the bar.

I keep on walking, threading among the "children" carrying books, wearing serious faces and the Ivy look.

And pause in front of Folwell hall, at the bottom of the steps to watch the latest edition of what we used to call the "Folwell Follies" when the pretty girls would come running down the steps at each class bell.

And they're still running down the steps, prettier than ever.

Guy Stanton Ford was president in my day and, as I pass the administration building, I go back to the Saturday morning when, in clipped, polished words, he proposed to the Board of Regents that they permit a woman named Sister Elizabeth Kenny to practice her methods of treating polio patients at the university.

The knoll is still there and the traffic circle, but where are the inter-campus streetcars and—what was his name—"Skipper" the grand old conductor who was as much a fixture as Burton Hall? Or the traffic cop—Herman Glander—whose friendly chatter and smile were part of an era when the parking problem was unknown.

And you'd walk across the knoll on a bitter, winter's morning, fighting the wind and cinders of locomotives rushing just below and beyond old Burton auditorium.

There was the young coed who left a lemon in my post office box one morning because I hadn't been able to stick around the day before and drink lemonade with her.

And I married the girl, finally.

These things I remember as I stroll the campus now, back along the mall, up the great steps into Northrop auditorium and my feet, suddenly, are those of a sober junior leaning into the wind on those very same steps the morning of Dec. 8, 1941, to hear—inside—the president of the university urge the student body to keep calm and stay at their books until they were called to go to war.

And just as I start down the spiral stairs to the post office in the basement of the Union, I remember the knot in the pit of my stomach when, just after each quarter ended, I would make that pilgrimage to the mailbox and opening it, slowly pick out the slip with my marks written down.

Then I stand on the wide concrete in front of the Union and watch the passing parade of youth. And suddenly I feel old and it all seems a long time ago.

As I watch them pass, the quick-stepping, laughing young freshmen, clean-cut, clear-eyed, I wonder if they feel that magic moment, four, five or six years hence will never come—as I did.

And I wish I could tell them so they'd understand that it will come sooner than they think.

That all the hours of preparing for exams, the nervous pacing, the anxious checking of notes will fade into fond memories one day and, like me, they will cross the stage once more and sing "Hail Minnesota" the last time and their university will become their alma mater because they hold a piece of paper in their hands.

[*Pillsbury and Burton Halls still stand, but Coffman Union has been totally transformed and the Memorial Stadium has been razed.*]

News Behind Bars—The Mirror on the St. Croix

One of Minnesota's pioneers of journalism had its 72nd birthday on August 10, 1959, yet there was little acclaim by its companions of the press and certainly no civic celebration.

But there may be a touch of pride in the birthday story the editor writes each year for his newspaper, the Stillwater *Prison Mirror*. For the *Mirror* holds the distinction of being the oldest continuously published prison newspaper in the United States.

And while I am happy to say that good newspapermen have been hard to find at Stillwater through the years and there certainly has been no beating upon the doors for employment, the administration has found it possible to maintain a high standard of newspapering.

The *Mirror* has never, for instance, been sued for libel. And its columns have provided an outlet for poets, philosophers, one of the present being a young man who writes a column entitled: "Fog on the St. Croix," though, ironically, neither author nor readers can quite see that picturesque valley just beyond the walls.

Through the years the *Mirror* has, at various times, been a sounding board for prisoners, but never a gripe sheet. Under the present direction of Warden Douglas C. Rigg, the paper is more nearly like the weeklies and dailies on the other side of the walls as it ever has been. A newspaper providing information of interest to prisoners about what is going on inside.

"The *Mirror*," says Warden Rigg, "is governed only by the dictates of truth and good taste."

Which, I might add, are sound dictates for any newspaper.

The unusual fact that the *Mirror* has become the dean of American prison journals is no more unusual than its inception on Aug. 10, 1887.

The paper was founded as a stock company, organized by a group of inmates who, with outside and legal connections, solicited ads from Stillwater merchants to pay the costs of publication.

"Dividends" came in the form of cash, used exclusively to buy books and periodicals for the prison library.

It is interesting to note that among the first investors were Coleman Younger, James Younger and Robert Younger—the Younger brothers, who in their day were some of the state's roughest.

These shareholders permitted prison officials to take part of their prison earnings and place them in a trust fund, the money to be repaid at 3 percent interest.

The project was launched on a flowery note. In its first issue, the paper was introduced by these phrases:

"The *Prison Mirror* casts its first reflections upon the world.

"And sheds a ray of light upon the lives of those behind the bars.

"Its founders, its mission. And its management."

In tribute to the warden of 1887, H. G. Stordock, the editor, Lew P. Schoonmaker, wrote:

"In thus extending to us the privilege of publishing and sending forth to the world the *Mirror*, our Warden has, we feel, extended to us a most elevating and beneficial privilege, which we trust, will be most fully appreciated and honored by each and every prisoner within our midst."

Under its nameplate, the *Mirror* that day carried this motto:

"God Helps Those Who Help Themselves."

And this almost caused the immediate demise of the paper.

For outsiders took violent exception to that motto, feeling that it was sacrilegious to intimate that the Divine Being would help anybody get to prison.

So the motto was quickly changed to: "It's Never too Late to Mend," which has remained unchanged to this day.

Unlike its outside counterparts, the *Mirror* cannot extend to the public a friendly invitation to drop in and "watch the presses roll." And not too many outsiders have been inside the *Mirror* office.

I spent more than an hour there some months ago, chatting with the editor, who wears a collegiate look and is a self-trained journalist. With him was his columnist and assistant, a studious young man.

Their office, located in the print shop, looks out on the grassy prison yard. And, except that you knew where you were, the scene and conversation that day were much like that in any newspaper office.

The proofs hanging on the hook, the chatter of the linotypes next door, and in one corner inmates—pressmen—putting that issue of the *Mirror* to bed.

Gathering and writing the news is a full time job for the editor and his assistant.

"I've got a regular news beat to cover like all reporters—I guess," he says. The "I guess" is inserted because the editor never was a newspaperman before he came to prison, though he'd like to try his hand when he gets out.

If prestige is measured by how much a newspaper is quoted by the other newspapers, the *Mirror* ranks high. Its gems have been reprinted around the world.

Probably the most quotable quote in its history belongs to the present editor, who one day covered a tour of the prison made by Governor Freeman.

As the party passed through a door the governor brushed the editor's sleeve.

"Pardon me," said the editor.

"Certainly," said Governor Freeman.

"But," wrote the editor sadly, "I didn't get it in writing."

Christmas Eve in the City

Along about 4:30 p.m. the lights begin to come on and a strange quiet muffles the city with the dusk.

And if you go up one of the seven hills of St. Paul and watch and listen, you feel the stillness of the city below on Christmas eve. Even in the chilly wind the warmth of this one night will rise off the forests of buildings.

In the now dim, almost empty aisles of the department stores on Wabasha and Robert, the fever of the weeks before has subsided. The white covers have been drawn over the confusion of the counters. Only the echoes of the shoppers' frenzy, the employees' parties at the end still ring faintly.

The people have long ago left the loop. In place of the 5 p.m. rush hour, the last trickle of the stream of humanity rides out on buses and cars, leaving only rows of parking meters like picket fences. The Minnesota Mutual chimes play to an empty house at 5 p.m.

There are gay, bright lights in the city tonight, but not from the flashing neon of the cafes and bars, night clubs or taverns. These, too, are dark. For tonight the lights belong to Christmas—to the lighted trees, shining out of mansion and hovel alike. Of decorations swinging in the night wind, spotlights bathing church steeples, which point like beacons into the darkness.

There is music in the city, too. For this night—at least—it is not rock 'n' roll or the discordant jangle of the music of an era or a generation. It is the music of the ages, rising in a crescendo from an organ in a church, from voices gathered around a piano, playing out of the radio in the cab that prowls the streets, on the desk of the hotel night clerk.

It is the tune that the patrolman hums to himself as he walks his beat along Jackson Street and the nun recalls from her childhood as she keeps her vigil in the corridors of St. Joseph's Hospital. And the soft caroling down the halls of Ancker Hospital drowns out the cries of anguish in the receiving room and the moan of the siren at the back door.

You hear it, too, reverberating through the vaulted Union depot concourse, played by the organ set in the center, a perfect background for the happy shouts of friends and families in arm-in-arm reunion at Gate 11 or 12 or 18. And down in the trainshed, in the half light of the limited's locomotive cab, the engineer opens his lunchbox and takes out a cold sandwich and whistles a Christmas tune as he recalls Christmas eves of his boyhood.

And I wonder if the pilot of the plane, winging across the city for a landing, imagines himself as something like a Santa Claus, bringing human gifts to people waiting in the terminal? Or does he sing "Jingle Bells" to himself?

And so you stand there on one of the seven hills of St. Paul and look across it on Christmas eve. Then you think how it is with some of the people hidden behind those lights.

There's Casey, the cab driver, taking people to midnight church services, and you know he won't have to spend Christmas in his lonely room. You wonder which of the many invitations to dinner he accepted—those that were phoned in to you.

You remember another lonely man, Father George Skluzacek, chaplain at the Carmelite convent at Lake Demontreville, and remember the care with which the Guild of Catholic Women packed his gifts while you watched a week ago. "He is one of our special people," they said.

For just a minute you think about Mrs. Gladys Weins, alone tonight at 1641 S. Concord, who took her widow's mite and turned it into Christmas cards for hundreds of men and women in prisons. And you remember the story you heard yesterday about Wilhelm Raade, Norwegian seafarer and artist, who brought his wife and 16-year-old daughter to the city and about the hopes he has that this will be the promised city for a 61-year-old artist, yet the dwindling cash in his pocket was not enough to buy them much of a Christmas for their little apartment. So their only friend in the city, a guy named Al Smith, took what little he had and gave it to them.

You'd like to look in, too, on the bare apartments and tattered houses and see the looks on the faces of all the children who will know Christmas is for them, too, because of the generosity of the city. A lot of those lights out there tonight are—halos being worn.

You have a thought, too, for a little girl named Shannon Neagle, who was 9 and didn't quite live to see the city tonight. Her funeral was yesterday. But the gift she left is as wonderful as any that will be given this year. Her illness created a bond of friendship among the families who live in Windward Heights No. 2. They learned the joy of unselfishness.

Suddenly, standing there on the hill, you know that word is the key to the way it is in the city tonight.

It is mirrored in the judge who will forsake his own Christmas dinner tomorrow to eat with the prisoners in the City Workhouse and talk with each of them.

It is the stranger you meet on the street corner tonight, who wishes you a "Merry Christmas" instead of passing without recognition. The cop who buys the transient a cup of coffee and finds him a bed at the Union Gospel Mission.

And so you walk back into the city, with only one regret. That it is like this in the city only once a year.

A car passes and the driver leans out and shouts, "Merry Christmas!"

"Merry Christmas!" you shout back. And it's meant for everybody.

Captain's Roost on Mounds Park

It was on one of those April-like December afternoons before Christmas when Ary Scheffer and I went back to review the strange but fascinating history of his old family home, a statuesque fortress that has commanded a stirring panorama of the city and valley for more than a century.

Even after 100 years, it stands—a sentinel of grandeur up there near the peak of the ridge leading into Mounds Park.

As I looked at it, catching the light of the sun's rays, it reminded me, too, of a white-gloved and haughty dowager perched on her throne.

The very site of this 15-room house has had an interesting past. For the old Scheffer place is perhaps the only dwelling in the city which has had three different addresses without moving a foot off its foundation.

In the beginning it was No. 52 Main, later 52 Bates and now is listed as 908 Mound.

It is, too, probably the only house in these parts which was ever raffled off for $5, then regained lost prestige and dignity to rise again in value.

You know how it is with so many old houses, not more than half the age of this one? They wear at the edges and fall. The floors sag, the paint peels and you approach them with a certain feeling of melancholia about what once was but is no longer.

But not the old Scheffer house. The crochet fringe has been removed from the cornices and porches, the vast acreage that once spread below it in terraces has been trimmed by residential encroachment.

But the old centenarian is as stout and trim and manicured today as it ever was—if not more so.

This is due wholly to a Mrs. Mildred Evans who, for a number of years, has operated it as the Mounds Park Rest home, taking care that the most modern conveniences and equipment be installed without destroying the heritage of the past.

You find, for instance, the latest all-steel cooking range in the kitchen, and across the hall a white marble mantelpiece around the fireplace in the living room, a mantelpiece delicately carved and immaculately maintained.

Though you can, from an attic window, still see west to the spires of downtown Minneapolis, south to Hastings, north across the St. Paul skyline and southwest straight up the Mississippi toward Fort Snelling, one unusual feature of the home, as it was built, has been destroyed.

The old steamboat pilothouse is gone.

And that takes the story back to the beginning and the building of No. 908 Mound.

It was not always the Scheffer place. In fact the span from 1886 to about 1899 when banker Albert Scheffer owned it was merely a phase of its long and colorful career.

A Commodore Davidson built the place in 1856. Like a lot of other steamboat captains and nautical persons who built houses along the Mississippi, he put his place at what he considered to be the best possible vantage for looking at the river. In addition, the commodore erected on the roof a glassed-in pilothouse.

The romantic beginnings seemed to follow the old house. Sometime in its life, the place was a military academy. And when, a few years ago, Mrs. Evans was remodeling the basement, she found initials of the "cadets" still carved in the woodwork.

There is, too, the story that Joe Rolette hid in the Scheffer home the papers that involved a plan to move the State Capitol from St. Paul to St. Peter.

And once, on a dark night, Ary Scheffer recalls that his mother heard digging near a tree in the yard and learned later that whoever had been shoveling at midnight was looking for supposedly buried treasure.

"We never found it, if it was or is there," said Ary.

In 1872, the house, having fallen into tarnished times, became part of a newspaper raffle and Dr. J. H. Murphy, well-known St. Paul physician, got it for a five-dollar bill.

The Scheffer reign began in 1886 and lasted until about the turn of the century. It was during this period that the yard boasted a fountain and artificial lake, and a long, winding, gravel driveway.

"It was a wonderful place in which to grow up," says Ary, referring to his own childhood and that of his four sisters, one of them the late Mrs. William Hamm, Sr., of the brewing family.

But the panic of the late 1890s took the house out of Ary's life and it took an erratic course until the early 1940s when Mrs. Evans moved in and restored it to present status.

And I think that this is one of the reasons why the house holds so much fascination for me. I have written about many an old building and landmark, but usually in a minor key, observing the demise or fall.

Not so with the old dowager up there on the ridge. She wears her pride as jauntily as any new home of style finished in the city within the last month.

Haunted House on Pleasant Avenue

Every town, hamlet, village and city worth its salt has, presently or in legend, a haunted house. Maybe a couple of them.

Never in fact, but always in fancy, these places are the scary delight of the youngsters and frequently their elders, though the latter would hardly admit it.

I have never found a census of St. Paul's haunted houses. But there is one dwelling whose ghostly history has mystery and the best in spooky fascination.

And it may come as a shock to the two families now living there to know that the house I mean still stands at No. 486 Pleasant, well beyond the Ramsey intersection.

The ghost or "hant" that inhabited that place—and it was seen all right—has probably long since passed into the middle distance.

But back in 1911, during February, the eyes of the city were on 486 Pleasant where Mrs. Emma Sebastian was frightened out of her wits by the meanderings of an ethereal man with a black mustache, furry coat and wearing moccasins.

The Sebastian ghost, strictly out of character, did not just prowl the halls and closets of the house during the dead of night. He stalked in broad daylight, so unnerving Mrs. Sebastian and her five children that they were on the fringe of hysteria when the world suddenly took notice.

In fact they moved.

But what added to the mystery of the home was the discovery, in the dirt basement floor, of bones, a crucifix and rosary.

That came when the investigation was well along and the case assumed sensational proportions. The case was, in fact, too much for the police.

Coroner Jones, at a nod from County Attorney O'Brien, called an inquest on the spot. But the bones, unfortunately, did not turn out to be human. Rather the panel of learned physicians decided that what had been unearthed were the bones of a well-boiled, well-eaten pig.

The presence of the rosary and crucifix was never explained, however, though the theory was advanced that they may have belonged to a pioneer settler, perhaps a French fur trader.

Which caused many "ghost experts" to jump to the conclusion that the Sebastian ghost was that fur trader come back for his possessions which he had left behind in his haste to get to the other world.

Many brave men and women came to tame the ghost. Some mothers brought their babies in carriages.

One of the bravest of them all was George Van Cook, a soldier with a record for bravery which he said he was "willing to stake on any ghost in St. Paul."

He volunteered to sit up one night to "get" the vanishing one or find out why.

"I have faced many an enemy in my fighting days," he said. "I am not afraid of this apparition."

Thus, at 9 p.m. on the dark and cloudless night of Feb. 18, old Indian fighter Van Cook, gun in hand, walked ramrod straight into the house and took up his vigil in one of the bedrooms which the ghost seemed to prefer.

All night he sat there and into the dawn, loaded for ghost. Nothing happened.

That more or less destroyed the spell and the Sebastian ghost kept attracting less and less attention until at last it was forgotten.

The incident, at its height, was not without some interesting sidelights.

Twin sisters threw the crowd into a tizzy one day. A small boy happened to see one twin, peeking through the keyhole of the front door. Then he ran around to the back and saw the other twin also peeking through the rear door.

Since the twins were dressed alike, the boy thought he'd seen a ghost. And it was some minutes before the thrill wore off.

Another lad, with fortitude, jumped down into the basement—through the outdoor window well. By then it was known as the "boogy-boogy."

Anxious bystanders saw him disappear into the dark reaches of the cellar where the bones had been found.

"He came out white as a sheet" and all waited for his pronouncement.

"Didn't see nuthin," he said. "But, boy am I scared."

The house at 486 Pleasant still looks much as it did then. The stone cellar is there, but the siding has been covered with shingles. And the house is in a paint-smelling state of upkeep.

The people who live there now are not acquainted with the Sebastian ghost. When the other day, I knocked on the second floor apartment door, I felt a little foolish.

How do you phrase the question: "Good afternoon, madam. Did you know your house was haunted? Heard anything odd lately?"

I feel lucky that the door was not slammed shut in my face, or that an alarm was not sent out for the men in white.

You can look and look all around outside. But as the little boy said when he came out of the "boogy-boogy,"

"You can't see nuthin."

THE END

When Gary Hiebert retired from the *Pioneer Press* in 1986, his colleague, long-time editorial cartoonist Jerry Fearing, saluted his departure. In a large ink drawing the artist depicted "Oliver Towne" as a writer who had begun work in St. Paul's long-ago cave days. Abandoning his computer, a jaunty "Oliver Towne" is shown heading for retirement in his skin apparel, hat, and carrying his briefcase.

Index